Advance Acclaim for
If Your Adolescent Has an Anxiety Disorder

"This book is a must for any parent who has an adolescent plagued by worries and anxiety. It is unique in combining current knowledge with practical information about what adolescents experience, what can be done, and how parents can help. Although written for parents, professionals will also benefit from the book's broad discussion of diagnosis, treatment, and causes of various anxiety states. Clearly, this book reflects the vast clinical experience of a seasoned and compassionate clinician."

—Rachel Klein, Ph.D., New York University Child Study Center

"In this marvelous book, Edna Foa takes pioneering work on anxiety and obsessive-compulsive disorders in adults and, in the context of the child and adolescent literature, applies it to children and adolescents and their families. Full of clinical wisdom and built on the best available evidence, the book will be an exceptionally valuable resource for families and for clinicians working with anxious youth. We can only hope that the state of clinical practice comes to reflect the standards of care outlined in this book. Highly recommended for professionals and nonprofessionals alike."

—John S. March, M.D., M.P.H., Professor and Chief, Child and Adolescent Psychiatry, Program for Child Affective & Anxiety Disorders, Duke University Child and Family Study Center

"Foa and Andrews provide parents a rich understanding of a variety of worries, fears, and anxieties, and they provide guidelines on how to help their teens overcome them. Parents will find the book engaging, easy to read, and full of important ideas about how best to understand and help their teens. A must read . . . for the teen's sake and ours."

—Thomas H. Ollendick, Ph.D., University Distinguished Professor and Director, Child Study Center, Virginia Tech

"Problems with anxiety can change the life course for many teenage children. Yet good and unbiased information is almost nonexistent. This book is written by two authors who are armed with a wealth of scientific information, extensive experience, and empathic understanding. Dr. Foa and Ms. Andrews provide a vital resource for parents of anxious teenagers. The language is clear and straightforward and the information is accurate and up-to-date. It is a book that every parent with an anxious teenager must have."

—Ronald M. Rapee, Ph.D., Director, Macquarie University Anxiety Research Unit, and Author of *Helping Your Anxious Child: A Step by Step Guide for Parents*

"An essential read, this book is a clear, concise, comprehensive resource for parents of children experiencing problems with anxiety."

—Louis Harkins, Founder and Administrator of the OCD and Parenting List

"Easy-to-read . . . an invaluable resource for parents and professionals alike. This volume can greatly assist parents as well as professionals to more effectively identify and help adolescents who are suffering. I would highly recommend it to parents as well as professional colleagues."

—Esther Deblinger, Ph.D., New Jersey CARES Institute, University of Medicine & Dentistry of N.J., School of Osteopathic Medicine

The Annenberg Foundation Trust at Sunnylands'
Adolescent Mental Health Initiative

Patrick Jamieson, Ph.D., *series editor*

Other books in the series

*If Your Adolescent Has Depression
or Bipolar Disorder (2005)*
Dwight L. Evans, M.D., and Linda Wasmer Andrews

If Your Adolescent Has an Eating Disorder (2005)
B. Timothy Walsh, M.D., and V. L. Cameron

If Your Adolescent Has Schizophrenia (2006)
Raquel E. Gur, M.D., Ph.D., and Ann Braden Johnson, Ph.D.

If Your Adolescent Has an Anxiety Disorder

An Essential Resource for Parents

- *Social Anxiety Disorder*
- *Generalized Anxiety Disorder*
- *Obsessive-Compulsive Disorder*
- *Post-Traumatic Stress Disorder*

Edna B. Foa, Ph.D., and Linda Wasmer Andrews

The Annenberg Foundation Trust at Sunnylands'
Adolescent Mental Health Initiative

THE ANNENBERG
PUBLIC POLICY CENTER
OF THE UNIVERSITY OF PENNSYLVANIA

OXFORD
UNIVERSITY PRESS

2006

OXFORD
UNIVERSITY PRESS

Oxford University Press, Inc., publishes works that
further Oxford University's objective of excellence
in research, scholarship, and education.

The Annenberg Foundation Trust at Sunnylands
The Annenberg Public Policy Center of the University of Pennsylvania
Oxford University Press

Oxford   New York
Auckland   Cape Town   Dar es Salaam   Hong Kong   Karachi
Kuala Lumpur   Madrid   Melbourne   Mexico City   Nairobi
New Delhi   Shanghai   Taipei   Toronto

With offices in
Argentina   Austria   Brazil   Chile   Czech Republic   France   Greece
Guatemala   Hungary   Italy   Japan   Poland   Portugal   Singapore
South Korea   Switzerland   Thailand   Turkey   Ukraine   Vietnam

Library of Congress Cataloging-in-Publication Data
Foa, Edna B.
If your adolescent has an anxiety disorder : an essential resource for
parents / Edna B. Foa and Linda Wasmer Andrews.
    p. cm. — (The Annenberg Foundation Trust at Sunnylands' adolescent
    mental health initiative)
"Social anxiety disorder, Generalized anxiety disorder, Obsessive-compulsive disorder,
Post-traumatic stress disorder."
Includes bibliographical references and index.
ISBN-13: 978-0-19-518151-7 (pbk-13)   ISBN-10: 0-19-518151-4 (pbk)
ISBN-13: 978-0-19-518150-0 (cloth-13)   ISBN-10: 0-19-518150-6 (cloth)
1. Anxiety in children. 2. Anxiety in children—Treatment. I. Andrews, Linda Wasmer.
II. Title. III. Series.
RJ506.A58F63 2006   618.92'8522—dc22   2005023770

9 8 7 6 5 4 3 2 1
Printed in the United States of America on acid-free paper

Contents

Six

Post-Traumatic Stress Disorder:
Failure to Recover From a Trauma   129

Seven

Treatment and Recovery:
A Close-Up of the Process   159

Eight

Call to Action: Fighting Stigma,
Empowering Your Teen   190

Foreword

The Adolescent Mental Health Initiative (AMHI) was created by The Annenberg Foundation Trust at Sunnylands to share with mental health professionals, parents, and adolescents the advances in treatment and prevention now available to adolescents with mental health disorders. The Initiative was made possible by the generosity and vision of Ambassadors Walter and Leonore Annenberg, and the project was administered through the Annenberg Public Policy Center of the University of Pennsylvania in partnership with Oxford University Press.

The Initiative began in 2003 with the convening, in Philadelphia and New York, of seven scholarly commissions made up of over 150 leading psychiatrists and psychologists from around the country. Chaired by Drs. Edna B. Foa, Dwight L. Evans, B. Timothy Walsh, Martin E. P. Seligman, Raquel E. Gur, Charles P. O'Brien, and Herbert Hendin, these commissions were tasked with assessing the state of scientific research on the prevalent mental disorders whose onset occurs predominantly between the ages of 10 and 22. Their collective findings now appear in a book for mental health professionals and policy makers titled *Treating and Preventing Adolescent Mental Health Disorders*

(2005). As the first product of the Initiative, that book also identified a research agenda that would best advance our ability to prevent and treat these disorders, among them anxiety disorders, depression and bipolar disorder, eating disorders, substance abuse, and schizophrenia.

The second prong of the Initiative's three-part effort is a series of books, including this one, that are designed primarily for parents of adolescents with a specific mental health disorder. Drawing their scientific information largely from the AMHI professional volume, these "parent books" present each relevant commission's findings in an accessible way and in a voice that we believe will be both familiar and reassuring to parents and families of an adolescent-in-need. In addition, this series, which will be followed by another targeted for adolescent readers themselves, combines medical science with the practical wisdom of parents who have faced these illnesses in their own children.

The third part of the Sunnylands Adolescent Mental Health Initiative consists of two websites. The first, www.CopeCare Deal.org, addresses teens. The second, www.oup.com/us/teenmentalhealth, provides updates to the medical community on matters discussed in *Treating and Preventing Adolescent Mental Health Disorders*, the AMHI professional book.

We hope that you find this volume, as one of the fruits of the Initiative, to be helpful and enlightening.

Patrick Jamieson, Ph.D.
Series Editor
Adolescent Risk Communication Institute
Annenberg Public Policy Center
University of Pennsylvania
Philadelphia, PA

If Your Adolescent Has an
Anxiety Disorder

Chapter One

Introduction: Uneasy Minds

One mother recalls that her son always seemed to be a little more fearful than most children. "But it really started interfering with his life when he was about 15. He began worrying constantly that his heart would stop beating while he was sleeping."

Another mother says that her daughter "was very, very introverted during her early teens. She avoided all public speaking, including talking in class. She was always too afraid to draw attention to herself in case she said or did something wrong."

A father says that his 16-year-old son became obsessed with a fear of contamination. Recently, the father was called to pick up the boy from school. The reason? "My son had dropped his lunch on the floor by accident. When he bent down to pick it up, the sleeve of his sweatshirt grazed the floor, and he became petrified. He told me later he just had to go home to 'sterilize' himself after that."

A grandmother says that her granddaughter continued to relive the horror of childhood sexual and physical abuse for years afterward. Once the abuse came to light, the girl went to live with her grandparents, where she had a safe, stable home. "But night was still a nightmare for us," her grandmother says. "She wasn't able to sleep for more than 45 minutes at a time. Then she would wake up screaming."

These stories sound quite different in some ways, but they all have a common thread running through them: anxiety.

1

In fact, each of these teenagers has been diagnosed with an anxiety disorder, one of a group of psychological disorders that lead to excessive or irrational anxiety, worry, and fear. On any given day, from 3% to 5% of children and adolescents in the United States have some type of anxiety disorder. Without treatment, this kind of disorder can interfere with their ability to carry out everyday tasks, succeed in school, or make and keep friends. Or it may simply cause great distress that saps much of their enjoyment from life.

On any given day, from 3% to 5% of children and adolescents in the United States have some type of anxiety disorder.

The parents quoted above also share a common bond: No matter how much or how little they already knew about anxiety disorders, all struggled to accept and understand what was happening when *their* child first became ill. "It was really scary," says the mother of the boy who feared his heart would stop beating. The fact that she is an experienced psychotherapist didn't change the anguish and helplessness she initially felt when it was her own son who was suffering.

If you've found yourself in a similar situation, chances are you know these feelings all too well. The good news is that we now know more about treating anxiety disorders than ever before. There aren't any miracle cures, but there are effective forms of psychotherapy and medication to help your teen feel better. As for your own feelings, we can't promise that the concerns and frustrations will totally disappear—after all, you're raising a teenager! But the worries should lessen as your teen's symptoms improve, and the sense of helplessness should fade as you take charge of the situation by finding treatment for your child and a support network for yourself.

How This Book Can Help

Perhaps you're just starting to wonder whether your teen might have an anxiety disorder. Or maybe you've already begun the process of seeking a diagnosis and treatment for your teen. In either case, this book provides the practical, reliable information you need to allay your concerns and empower yourself as a parent.

"Anxiety disorder" is an umbrella term that covers seven different conditions: social anxiety disorder, generalized anxiety disorder (GAD), obsessive-compulsive disorder (OCD), post-traumatic stress disorder (PTSD), separation anxiety disorder, panic disorder, and specific phobias. In this book, we'll be focusing mainly on the first four, because those are the anxiety disorders that lead to the most trouble during adolescence. By contrast, panic disorder usually begins in adulthood, while separation anxiety and specific phobias are more prominent in childhood and usually lessen during adolescence.

Of the four disorders highlighted in this book

- Social anxiety disorder is quite prevalent, and it typically begins in late childhood or early adolescence.
- GAD is also common, affecting at least 2% of all adolescents.
- OCD is less common, but the symptoms can be especially disruptive to the lives of young people.
- PTSD can lead to particularly distressing symptoms as well. In addition, adolescents are at higher risk than other age groups for many of the traumatic events that can give rise to PTSD.

The causes, symptoms, and treatments of social anxiety disorder, GAD, OCD, and PTSD will be described in detail in the chapters to come. Of course, you may be curious about separation anxiety disorder, panic disorder, and specific phobias, too. If nothing else, you may have heard these terms tossed around casually and wonder what they really mean, scientifically speaking. So we've also provided briefer descriptions of these three disorders in Chapter 2.

Throughout the book, you'll find straightforward, scientifically sound answers to the questions that parents of teens with anxiety disorders most often ask. For example:

- What's the difference between everyday anxiety and an anxiety disorder?
- If my teen has an anxiety disorder, is it my fault?
- What are the warning signs to watch for?
- What type of therapy helps with anxiety disorders?
- What are the pros and cons of medication?
- Will insurance cover the costs of treatment?
- How can I help my teen succeed in school?
- What does the future hold for my teen?
- Where can I find further support and education for myself?

No book can take the place of professional diagnosis and treatment by a qualified mental health care provider. But this book can arm you with the facts you need in order to choose a qualified professional in the first place. And once you've found the right person to provide a diagnosis and treatment, this book can help you and your teen make the most of that opportunity. The more you know, the better equipped you'll be to ask critical questions, make informed decisions, and, when necessary, advocate for your teen effectively with the insurance company or school system.

The more you know, the better equipped you'll be to ask critical questions, make informed decisions, and, when necessary, advocate for your teen.

How This Book Is Organized

In Chapter 2 of this book, you'll find an introduction to all seven types of anxiety disorders. Here's where you'll learn what distinguishes one disorder from another and why they all represent some form of dysfunctional anxiety. If you've ever wondered what a phobia or panic attack really is, this chapter will help you clarify the true meaning of these widely used—but sometimes misused—terms.

In Chapters 3 through 6, you'll find in-depth discussions of the four anxiety disorders that are especially relevant to adolescents: social anxiety disorder, generalized anxiety disorder (GAD), obsessive-compulsive disorder (OCD), and posttraumatic stress disorder (PTSD). These chapters describe the symptoms, risk factors, causes, diagnosis, and treatments of each disorder. They also discuss ways that parents can help with the day-to-day management of symptoms at home and school. Since you may just want to read about your own teen's disorder, we've made sure that each of these chapters can stand alone as a guide to that particular condition. You can skip the chapters that don't apply to your teen. Or if you prefer to read the book straight through, you can skip the few sections that are, of necessity, repeated from one chapter to the next. In particular, the section called Medication Therapy is similar for all the disorders. You might want to read through it once carefully and then skim over it in the remaining chapters.

In Chapter 7, you'll find a close-up look at treatment and recovery issues that are relevant to all kinds of anxiety disorders. There's a general discussion of the pros and cons of therapy and medication as well as suggestions for helping your teen get the most benefit from whatever treatment option is chosen. In addition, there are practical pointers on dealing with managed care companies and your teen's school.

In Chapter 8, we tie things up with suggestions for standing up to stigma and empowering your teen. At the back of the book, you'll find an appendix of diagnostic criteria, a glossary, and a list of additional resources you may want to consult. All in all, we've tried to provide the information that a concerned, involved parent is most likely to need.

We've tried to paint a realistic portrait of what it's really like to raise an adolescent with an anxiety disorder. At times, you may feel stressed-out, worried, confused, frustrated, discouraged—or all of the above. There's no denying that your role as a mom or dad can be a very challenging one. Ultimately, though, there are many good reasons for feeling optimistic. Excellent treatments, including specifically targeted therapies and new medications, are now available, and most teens with anxiety disorders can be helped to feel better. You can play a pivotal role in that process by supporting your teen at home and seeking professional care when it's needed.

> Excellent treatments, including specifically targeted therapies and new medications, are now available, and most teens with anxiety disorders can be helped to feel better.

The People Behind the Book

In 2003, the Adolescent Mental Health Initiative, a project spearheaded by the Annenberg Foundation Trust at Sunnylands, convened a blue-ribbon commission of the nation's leading authorities on adolescent anxiety disorders. The result was a professional report that summarized the state of the science in this area. The book in your hands draws heavily on the commission's report to present you with the most up-to-date, authoritative information currently available.

The lead author of this book was chair of the commission. Dr. Foa is a professor of clinical psychology in psychiatry at the University of Pennsylvania, where she also directs the Center for the Treatment and Study of Anxiety. She is internationally recognized for her research on the causes and treatment of anxiety disorders, including OCD, PTSD, and social anxiety disorder. A therapeutic program she developed for trauma victims has been highly influential in the treatment of PTSD. Dr. Foa has published several books and over 250 articles and book chapters, and she has lectured extensively around the world. Over the years, she has received many honors, including an honorary doctorate from the University of Basel in Switzerland and the Distinguished Scientist Award and Distinguished Scientific Contributions to Clinical Psychology Award, both from the American Psychological Association.

Two of Dr. Foa's colleagues at the University of Pennsylvania contributed their considerable insights and expertise to this book as well. Martin E. Franklin, Ph.D., is an associate professor of clinical psychology in psychiatry at the University of Pennsylvania School of Medicine and clinical director of the Center for the Treatment and Study of Anxiety. Moira A. Rynn, M.D., is an assistant professor of psychiatry and medical director of the Mood and Anxiety Disorders Section at the University of Pennsylvania School of Medicine. We would like to express our appreciation to Dr. Franklin and Dr. Rynn for their help in reviewing and providing feedback on the scientific dimensions of the book.

The second author of this book is a journalist who has specialized in mental health issues for more than two decades. Her most important contribution to the project was to interview parents of adolescents with anxiety disorders from across the United States and beyond. These mothers and fathers—and one grandmother who is raising her granddaughter—generously shared their experiences, because they know how powerful parent-to-parent support can be. Many also passed along no-nonsense, hands-on advice about dealing with some of the thorniest parenting dilemmas you're likely to encounter. Names of parents and teens have been changed throughout the book in order to protect the families' privacy. But the stories are true, and the quotes from parents have an immediacy and authenticity that reflect the day-to-day reality of their lives—and perhaps your life, too. We think you'll find the parents' honesty, encouragement, and down-to-earth suggestions especially helpful.

Chapter Two

Anxiety Disorders: What They Are, Where They Come From

Believe it or not, anxiety is actually a good thing. Anxiety involves anticipating future danger or misfortune, and the ability to look ahead and think about future events is part of what makes us human. In reasonable doses, this capacity for forethought is protective. It's what keeps us from driving 90 miles per hour on an icy road or walking late at night in a dangerous neighborhood.

But when anxiety becomes extreme or irrational, it can quickly turn from adaptive to maladaptive. At this point, anxiety starts to cause considerable emotional distress and interfere with a person's ability to get along in everyday life. A number of intensely unpleasant mental, physical, and behavioral symptoms may also accompany the general sense of apprehension. The person has just crossed the threshold from "normal" anxiety to an anxiety disorder.

No two stories of teen anxiety are exactly the same.

Three Snapshots of Anxiety

No two stories of teen anxiety are exactly the same. The teenagers described below, along with

9

those in the rest of the book, have all been diagnosed with one or more anxiety disorders. Yet the way they experience the disorder is as uniquely individual as they are. Since these are real-life teens, not textbook cases, they don't always display the most common symptoms. But as a group, the teens described in this book do offer a true-to-life glimpse at the wide range of forms and severity that anxiety disorders can assume.

Kayla

Thirteen-year-old Kayla has an upstairs bedroom in her two-story house. One night recently, Kayla was in bed when she suddenly cried out for her mother. Alarmed, her mother, Liz, went immediately to see what was wrong. "I asked, 'What's the matter?' And she said, 'It sounds like somebody's whispering outside my window.'" Of course, it was just a tree branch making a scratching sound. Kayla acknowledged that it was highly unlikely that someone would actually be outside a second-story window. Yet she kept insisting, "I *feel* like somebody's there."

Kayla also tends to worry a lot about spending the night away from home. This is an issue that she and her mother have been working on with the help of her therapist. In seventh grade, Kayla's class was set to go on a weekend trip to a nearby city, and she seemed very excited about the prospect. But two days before the trip, Liz's cell phone rang soon after she had dropped Kayla off at school. It was her daughter saying that she had just thrown up and needed to go home because she was sick. Liz says, "I turned the car around, went back and got her, and took her home, where she didn't vomit again the whole rest of the day. She seemed fine."

The next day, the same thing happened again. Liz returned to the school once more, but this time she spent several minutes talking with her daughter. "I told her, 'I don't think you have the flu, because if you did, you wouldn't throw up only when you got to school.'" Mother and daughter agreed that the true culprit was probably anxiety. A year earlier, a quick pep talk wouldn't have been enough to reassure Kayla, but she had been making steady progress at controlling her anxiety since starting treatment. After talking the situation out, Kayla returned to school, and ultimately she went on the trip the next day. Says Liz, "She was very anxious at night, but a couple of her favorite teachers were chaperoning, which helped. She got through it and actually had a lot of fun." For Kayla, the trip represented a major victory.

Lucas

Around the time Lucas hit puberty, his behavior began to grow increasingly bizarre. "In our kitchen, we have a coffeemaker, a microwave, and a stove, and all three have clocks on them," says his mother, Ellen. She noticed her son standing by the clocks and muttering something to himself. Finally, she asked him what he was saying. "It turns out he was repeating the time backward and forward, over and over again. And if the times didn't match perfectly, it just drove him crazy. After a while, we unplugged everything, because it was getting so out of hand."

Not long afterward, Lucas began slapping his leg while muttering to himself. Ellen later learned that he was repeating a prayer backward and forward. "He was doing it so much that he had bruises on his leg," his mother says. "He tried to explain it to me, but all he could say was, 'I just can't help myself.' And then he cried, and he said, 'I can't stop!'" Fortunately, by this time Lucas was already in treat-

> He tried to explain it to me, but all he could say was, "I just can't help myself."

ment, which soon helped him manage to stop this behavior after all.

Troublesome new behaviors continue to crop up from time to time, however. Currently, "he washes his hands way too much," Ellen says. "He denies that he does it, but his hands are always red and cracked." For Lucas, who is now nearly 15 years old, treatment has greatly reduced his emotional distress, but the challenge of dealing with his compulsive behavior is still a work in progress.

Tim

When Tim was four years old, his mother married her second husband. A single mother with three young boys and a fourth baby on the way, Susan hoped the marriage would be a fresh beginning and bring much-needed stability to all their lives. Instead, the marriage got off to a tragic start when her fourth son died in his sleep at two months of age. Susan discovered the baby lying lifeless in his crib the next morning, and "my other children now tell me they remember waking up to my screams that day."

In the coming years, two more children were born, and the demands of raising her growing brood often left Susan feeling exhausted and overwhelmed. Meanwhile, the trauma within the family was compounded as Susan's husband grew increasingly volatile and abusive. Tim and his brothers were mercilessly belittled, while their mother bore the brunt of her husband's physical rage. She says he beat her frequently and threatened to kill her on at least two occasions, once with an ax and another time with a shotgun. At the time, Susan told herself that the children were sheltered from the worst of the violence. However, after she and her husband separated when Tim was 15 years old, Susan learned that her son had been more traumatized by the abuse than she had wanted to admit.

Today, it has been four years since the marriage ended, but Susan and her children are still dealing with the aftermath of the trauma. Tim, in particular, has had lingering problems with anxiety. One night recently, for instance, mother and son were watching a TV crime show about a murdered baby. "It was like it triggered something in Tim," Susan says. "He just got up suddenly, said, 'I can't watch this,' and left the room. I felt really bad, because he seemed so upset."

Tim doesn't like to talk much about the past, but his mother thinks she can see the residual effects in the recurring nightmares about his baby brother's death that have plagued him for years. Susan convinced Tim to see a therapist for a while, but he soon quit. His mother would like to see him back in treatment, though. "Tim tends to withdraw into himself and not share his feelings with anyone," she says. "It worries me. I'm afraid that if he doesn't get help and deal with what he's been through, all these feelings are going to hit him smack in the face one day."

Seven Types of Anxiety Disorders

As these vignettes illustrate, anxiety can take a wide variety of forms. Mental health professionals have divided anxiety disorders into seven major categories. Each category has its own set of characteristic signs and symptoms. Following are brief descriptions of the disorders. For a simplified version of the formal diagnostic criteria for each disorder, see the Appendix.

Social Anxiety Disorder

The defining characteristic of social anxiety disorder—also called social phobia—is marked fear in social situations where the person is exposed to unfamiliar people or possible scrutiny by others. While the disorder bears some similarity to ordinary shyness, the symptoms are more extreme and disabling. Young people with social anxiety disorder are capable of having age-appropriate relationships under certain circumstances; for instance, when visiting with a few, close friends in their own home. However, in less familiar or secure social situations, they worry excessively about possible ridicule, humiliation, or embarrassment. This anxiety can lead to severe distress or interfere with everyday activities and relationships.

Social anxiety disorder typically starts in late childhood or early adolescence. For some teens, the problem is limited to specific situations; for example, when speaking in class or eating in front of strangers. For other teens, though, it's more generalized, leading them to avoid a whole array of social situations. Social anxiety disorder is described at greater length in Chapter 3.

Generalized Anxiety Disorder (GAD)

As its name implies, GAD refers to excessive anxiety and worry over a number of things, such as schoolwork, appearance, health, money, and the future. At times, an unreasonable amount of worry may be focused on specific situations or events; for example, a good student might worry incessantly about grades. At other times, the worry isn't directed at anything in particular, but the person might nevertheless feel tense and uneasy all the time. The pattern of constant worrying lasts for a period of months or years, and the worrisome thoughts are hard to control.

Other symptoms of GAD include restlessness, fatigue, irritability, muscle tension, trouble concentrating, and difficulty falling or staying asleep. Although full-blown GAD sometimes doesn't develop until adolescence or later, many people with the disorder remember having felt anxious and nervous all their lives. GAD is described at greater length in Chapter 4.

Table 1. Lions and Tigers and Bears

Young people with anxiety disorders worry about many of the same things as other teens, but they just do so more frequently and intensely. In a study published in the *Journal of Abnormal Child Psychology* in 2000, 119 children and adolescents who were being seen at an anxiety disorders clinic were asked about what worried them most. Following are their top responses.

	Most frequent worries	*Most intense worries*
1	Friends	War
2	Classmates	Personal harm
3	School	Disasters
4	Health	School
5	Performance	Family

Adapted from Weems, C. F., Silverman, W. K., and La Greca, A. M. (2000). "What do youth referred for anxiety problems worry about? Worry and its relation to anxiety and anxiety disorders in children and adolescents." *Journal of Abnormal Child Psychology* 28, 63-72.

Obsessive-Compulsive Disorder (OCD)

The essential feature of OCD is the presence of uncontrollable obsessions or compulsions. Obsessions are recurrent thoughts that are intrusive and perceived as inappropriate by the person having them, and that provoke considerable anxiety and distress. Compulsions are repetitive behavioral or mental acts that a person feels driven to perform in response to an obsession or according to rigid rules. Such compulsions are aimed at preventing or reducing distress or preventing some dreaded event, even though there may be no realistic connection between the action and the feared situation.

Many teens with OCD realize that their recurrent thoughts and acts are excessive and unreasonable. Yet they feel unable to stop them. Some are obsessed with concerns about dirtiness or sinfulness. Others devote hours to compulsive behaviors, such as washing their hands, repeating actions a set number of times, or repeating words silently. OCD was once considered a rare condition in children and adolescents. However, research suggests that as many as 1% of young people may have the disorder. OCD is described at greater length in Chapter 5.

Post-Traumatic Stress Disorder (PTSD)

The thing that sets PTSD apart is that it is the only anxiety disorder that requires a precipitating event. In PTSD, the symptoms always develop following exposure to a traumatic occurrence. The event gives rise to intense feelings of fear, helplessness, or horror, because it is perceived as posing a threat to the physical integrity of oneself or others. For example, the seeds of PTSD might be sown when a person has a serious accident, becomes the victim of childhood sexual abuse, or witnesses a murder. Afterward, the person relives the trauma over and over in some way; for example, through flashbacks, nightmares, or recurring mental images.

People with PTSD try to avoid things or places associated with the trauma. Many also feel emotionally numb in situations that call for an emotional response. In addition, people with PTSD develop signs of heightened arousal, such as difficulty falling asleep, increased irritability, constant vigilance, or an exaggerated response when startled. It is as if the person's body is always on high alert, and the tension can be overwhelming. PTSD is described at greater length in Chapter 6.

Separation Anxiety Disorder

Unlike the four conditions discussed above, separation anxiety disorder is primarily found in younger children. It involves excessive anxiety about being separated from the parent or home. The degree of anxiety is developmentally inappropriate, and it causes undue distress or interferes with everyday activities. It's estimated that as many as 4% of children and young adolescents suffer from this disorder. However, the problem often fades away as the individuals get older.

Young people with separation anxiety disorder may worry incessantly about harm coming to a parent or about some untoward event that would lead to separation, such as getting lost or being kidnapped. In addition, they may be fearful about sleeping away from home, and they may develop physical complaints, such as headaches or an upset stomach, in anticipation of spending time away. In some children, separation anxiety takes the form of extreme reluctance to go to school. This, in turn, can lead to academic and social problems. When teenagers refuse to go to school, their behavior may sometimes be due to separation anxiety as well. However, there are more likely explanations at this age, including social anxiety disorder.

Panic Disorder

The hallmark of panic disorder is the occurrence of spontaneous panic attacks, which are sudden waves of intense fear and apprehension. These feelings are accompanied by physical symptoms, such as a rapid heart rate, shortness of breath, choking sensations, or sweating. The problem sometimes starts with sporadic, isolated attacks around the time of puberty. Over time, the attacks may gradually become more frequent, and those affected may grow increasingly worried about when and where the next attack will occur or what the consequences might be. Some may worry that they'll "lose their mind" or have a heart attack. However, this transition to full-blown panic disorder usually doesn't occur until late adolescence or early adulthood.

In adults, panic disorder is often associated with agoraphobia. The word "agoraphobia" literally means "fear of the marketplace." However, the term has taken on a broader meaning:

fear of being in places or situations from which escape might be difficult or in which help might not be available in the event of a panic attack. The fear typically extends across a wide swath of situations. In severe cases, the person becomes fearful of all situations in which they are outside their home alone or caught in a crowd. The intense anxiety aroused by these situations makes people want to avoid them. Some people force themselves to face the dreaded situations, but only at the expense of great distress. Others become virtually housebound.

Specific Phobias

A specific phobia is an intense fear that is out of proportion to any real threat and focused on a specific animal, object, activity, or situation. People with phobias experience anxiety when they encounter or even think about the thing they fear. This anxiety sometimes takes the form of a panic attack. But whereas the attacks in panic disorder seem to come out of the blue, the attacks in specific phobia have very specific triggers. The triggers themselves can be divided into five basic categories: animal (for example, dogs, mice, spiders), natural environment (for example, heights, water, storms), injury (for example, blood, injections), situational (for example, airplanes, elevators, enclosed spaces), and other (for example, choking, loud noises). When the trigger is situational, it's limited to a specific situation, rather than a whole cluster of situations as in agoraphobia.

Most of us have an irrational fear or two. To qualify as a specific phobia, however, the fear must lead to extreme distress or interfere with the ability to carry out normal activities. Such phobias are most common in childhood or early adolescence. They may follow a traumatic event involving the feared thing, an unexpected panic attack in the feared situation, the observation of fearfulness in others, or repeated parental warnings or media coverage about a certain hazard. People frequently find ways of avoiding their triggers. Unfortunately, this avoidance may impair their ability to function in daily life. For example, a mild fear of dogs is not uncommon. However, a teen with a phobia of the animals may be so intensely fearful that he won't venture outside his home for fear of encountering an unleashed dog.

About One Out of Every 20 Teens

Up to 5% of children and adolescents have an anxiety disorder on any given day. Although the nature of the anxiety may change, the prevalence rate stays about the same throughout childhood and adolescence. Girls are more likely than boys to have an anxiety disorder, and they also have a higher rate of referral for treatment. The reasons for this sex difference are still uncertain. However, sex hormones may play a role. Estrogen, a female hormone, is known to interact with serotonin, a brain chemical that has been implicated in both anxiety and depression.

Some studies of anxiety disorders have also found a stronger genetic influence in females than males. Societal expectations and stereotypes may play a role as well. For example, among adults, females are three times as likely as males to develop panic disorder with agoraphobia. One theory is that females may tend to deal with their anxiety about future panic attacks by avoiding the threatening situations. Males, on the other hand, may be more likely to feel as if they have to confront their fears, perhaps with the aid of alcohol or other drugs.

From Anxiety to Disorder

Anxiety disorders occur in people of all ages. However, the typical nature of the anxiety varies across different developmental stages. For young children, parents and home are the center of their universe, and a little anxiety about separation is perfectly normal. It's not surprising, then, that *excessive* separation anxiety is also most common at this stage. As children enter adolescence, relationships with peers become increasingly important. At the same time, adolescents are growing more self-aware, which means they are also more prone to painful self-consciousness. Not coincidentally, this is the stage at which *excessive* social anxiety typically starts.

Think back to how you felt on your first date. Maybe your palms were clammy and sweaty, or your stomach was filled with butterflies. This kind of nervousness is a normal reaction to a new experience—and when you're young, newness is the order of the day. For some young people, however, the feeling doesn't fade. They are plagued by persistent doubts and worries, and their distress may become so excruciating that they start to avoid any situation that might provoke it.

Eventually, this avoidance begins to interfere with their ability to function at home or school. Take the example of a teenage boy who experiences more than the usual amount of anxiety around girls. At first, he may simply avoid talking to girls in class for fear that he will somehow embarrass himself. As the anxiety mushrooms, however, he begins to dread going to school at all. By this point, the anxiety is clearly getting in the way of his social and academic life.

Distress and dysfunction are two of the cardinal signs that a person has crossed the line from ordinary anxiety to an anxiety disorder. The third is inflexibility—the inability to recover from anxiety-provoking situations and adapt emotionally to them. These are three important clues that mental health professionals consider when assessing whether an anxiety disorder is present.

As a parent, you have the immense advantage of knowing what's normal and what's not for your own child. If something seems seriously wrong, don't be afraid to ask for help. "In hindsight, I would trust my gut earlier than I did," says the mother of a girl who developed OCD at age 13. "I wouldn't wait for a teacher to confirm that she was having a problem when I could see it for myself." As with any other illness, the sooner an anxiety disorder is diagnosed and treated, the faster the suffering can begin to be relieved.

If something seems seriously wrong, don't be afraid to ask for help.

First Steps

As a parent, your first instinct is to protect and problem-solve, and there's nothing worse than feeling helpless to ease your child's worry and fear. You want to *do* something, but maybe you aren't sure where to start. Here's some advice from parents who have traveled the road before you.

- *Talk about it.* Don't be afraid to start a frank discussion with your teen. "I could tell something was going on with my son, but he never talked about it," says a father who has OCD himself. "So I opened up to him about my own experiences, and that's when he admitted that he was experiencing some similar things that he didn't understand."

- *Find a specialist.* Not all mental health professionals are equally familiar with the unique needs of teens with anxiety disorders. If possible, look for someone who specializes in the area. "We had to drive 45 minutes each way to the therapist, but it was worth it," says one mother. For more suggestions on finding a qualified treatment provider, see Chapter 7.

- *Educate yourself.* Professional help may be invaluable, but it doesn't take the place of doing your own homework. Read books, surf reputable websites, join a parent support group. Says one mother, "The more you know, the better off your child will be."

Coexisting Conditions

Mental health professionals use strict criteria to divide the anxiety disorders into distinct types for diagnostic and research purposes. This creates an illusion of neat, orderly categories. Real life is much messier than that, however. A teen who suffers from extreme anxiety in social situations might also have an irrationally intense fear of spiders as well as occasional panic attacks that seem to occur out of nowhere.

The term "comorbidity" is scientific jargon for the coexistence of two or more disorders in the same individual. There is a high level of comorbidity among teens with anxiety disorders, and this can complicate diagnosis and treatment. Yet, to get the best possible outcome for a particular teen, it's essential that any coexisting problems be recognized and treated in their own right.

Comorbidity with Other Disorders

Anxiety disorders can occur alongside other mental or behavioral disorders as well. Following are brief descriptions of some of the most common coexisting conditions.

- Depression—There is a very strong association between anxiety disorders and depression. Clinically speaking, depression is a mood disorder that involves either being depressed or irritable nearly all the time, or losing interest or enjoyment in almost everything. These feelings last for at least two weeks, are associated with other mental and physical symptoms, and cause significant distress or impaired functioning. Young people with anxiety disorders are eight times more likely than those without the disorders to suffer from depression. There may be a sequential link between the two conditions as well. Individuals who had an anxiety disorder in childhood have an increased risk of developing depression later in life.

- Substance abuse—The relationship between anxiety disorders and substance abuse is less clear-cut. Several studies have reported a significant association between the two problems. But a recent analysis suggests that, rather than a direct relationship, it might be an indirect one based on a common denominator, such as depression. There is also conflicting evidence on the link between early anxiety and later substance abuse. Researchers found that children who suffered from separation anxiety were less likely than other children to begin drinking alcohol as they grew older, and those who did drink tended to start at a later-than-average age. On the other hand, children with GAD were more likely to begin drinking and did so earlier in adolescence.

- Tic disorders—A tic is a sudden, rapid, repetitive movement or vocalization, such as repeated head jerking, facial grimacing, eye blinking, or throat clearing. Between 20% and 30% of people with OCD report having had tics at some point. A smaller number have full-fledged Tourette's syndrome, a neurological disorder characterized by frequent, multiple tics.

Luis's Story

"The Tourette's started when Luis was about six," recalls his mother. Over the years, the tics took a number of forms, including blinking, grimacing, sniffing, grunting, and whistling. But when Luis reached sixth grade, something changed. "We had mice in our crawl space, and he had heard somewhere that mice carry hantavirus," his mother says. "He became obsessed with the idea that he was going to die from hantavirus and go straight to hell." Thoughts of eternal damnation kept Luis awake at nights, and compulsive praying began to occupy more and more of his days. Luis's mother and doctor soon realized what was happening: Tourette's had been joined by OCD.

Labels and More Labels

Getting the right diagnosis—or diagnoses, in many cases—is important, because it helps medical and mental health professionals make the best treatment choices. In many cases, it's also a necessary step to obtaining insurance coverage or qualifying your teen for a special school program. However, it's crucial to remember that no labels can ever sum up the totality of your one-of-a-kind teen.

. . . no labels can ever sum up the totality of your one-of-a-kind teen.

Physicians, therapists, and teachers are occasionally guilty of tunnel vision. Some may have trouble seeing beyond a particular medical, psychological, or educational diagnosis. As a parent, though, you're more likely to see your child as a whole individual, much more than the sum of his or her labels. This is an extremely valuable perspective that you bring to your teen's situation. One mother whose 13-year-old son has been diagnosed with OCD, Tourette's syndrome, attention-deficit/hyperactivity disorder, and a learning disability put it this way: "He's been called a lot of things. But to me, he's just the same boy I've always raised and loved."

The Psychology of Anxiety

What causes anxiety to spiral out of control? That may be a straightforward, obvious question, but the answer is neither simple nor completely clear at this point. For one thing, the state we call "anxiety" encompasses a range of thoughts, feelings, and behaviors. It only stands to reason that a multifaceted state would have multiple causes. Among other things, anxiety seems to be influenced by psychological, biological, and genetic factors.

Classical Conditioning

One of the first scientific theories of anxiety was based on the assumption that phobias are acquired through classical conditioning. An association is formed by pairing a previously neutral stimulus (such as a bell) with an unconditioned stimulus (such as an electrical shock) to produce an unconditioned response (such as fear). Over time, the previously neutral stimulus, now called the conditioned stimulus, becomes able to bring on the fear all by itself.

In a 1920 paper that became one of the most-cited experiments in the history of psychology, John B. Watson and an associate showed how these same principles could be applied to conditioning fear in an 11-month-old boy named Albert. At first, the boy showed no fear of a white rat toy (neutral stimulus), but he cried and was startled (unconditioned response) when the researchers made a loud noise by hitting a steel bar with a hammer (unconditioned stimulus). Then the researchers began making the sound every time they showed the boy the white rat toy. Before long, the mere sight of the rat (conditioned stimulus) was enough to bring on crying (conditioned response). Not only that, but the boy's newly conditioned fear also generalized to other furry objects, including a dog, a rabbit, a fur coat, and even a Santa Claus mask.

As poor Albert demonstrated, fears can be learned through classical conditioning. According to learning theory, it follows that they can also be unlearned through extinction, in which the conditioned stimulus is presented repeatedly without the unconditioned stimulus. Over time, this leads to a weakening of the conditioned response, until it may disappear altogether.

Mental Processing

While conditioning is one piece of the puzzle, it ignores a crucial factor: the individual's ability to think about and attach personal meaning to an event or situation. More recent theories emphasize that it is not the event itself, but the way the event is perceived that determines how much fear it evokes. If a person interprets an event as threatening, then it is likely to arouse anxiety. Cognitive-behavioral therapy (CBT) builds on this concept. It teaches people how to put their interpretations to the reality test, then replace inaccurate thinking with more accurate views of the situation.

In 1986, this book's lead author and her colleague Michael J. Kozak proposed a new theory to explain anxiety disorders and their treatment. Called Emotional Processing Theory, it defines fear as a mental structure that serves as a blueprint for escaping or avoiding danger. Different anxiety disorders reflect different blueprints. For example, the fear structure of people with panic disorder is characterized by inaccurate interpretations of harmless bodily sensations as dangerous. When such people experience the rapid heart rate, shortness of breath, sweating, and other physical changes that go hand-in-hand with panicky feelings, they misinterpret these sensations as signs of a serious illness, such as a heart attack. As a result, they start avoiding situations that might give rise to future panic attacks. They may also avoid other things, such as vigorous exercise, that produce similar physical sensations.

In contrast, the fear structure of people with OCD is most often characterized by erroneous interpretations of safe things as being dangerous. For example, a harmless stain might be seen as evidence of contamination with deadly bacteria. But as with panic disorder—and as with other anxiety disorders, too—

the core problem is a faulty connection between stimuli and responses as well as a misinterpretation of the meaning of events.

Experimental studies support the notion that anxious youngsters are biased toward seeing threat where there is none or where the situation is ambiguous. In one group of studies, children and teens heard or read homophones—words that sound alike, but have different meanings. The particular homophones used in these studies (e.g., "whipping," "hang") each had a threatening meaning and a nonthreatening one. When asked to indicate the meaning of each word, the anxious youngsters were more likely than their nonanxious peers to go with the threatening option.

The Biology of Anxiety

Puberty is a time of rapid physical growth and maturation. You're aware when your daughter needs her first bra or your son outgrows his new shoes within weeks. Less visible but at least as important are the dramatic changes that are occurring within your teen's brain. Among other things, there are changes in brain circuitry, including the circuits involved in the recognition and expression of fear, anxiety, and other emotions. It is as if the brain is reinventing itself. One consequence of this major restructuring is that vulnerabilities that previously lay hidden may suddenly be exposed.

"My daughter's OCD became really full-blown right at the onset of puberty," says one mother. "My son stopped being so hyper, but the anxiety took a sharp turn for the worse when he was around 13," says another. For some young people, the transition from childhood to adolescence is fraught with new anxieties and worries. There are any number of possible explanations—everything from the pressures of middle school to the burgeoning of sexuality. However, it's worth noting that another likely contributor is the restructuring that is going on inside the brain.

Physiology of Fear

Scientists have been working to pinpoint the exact brain regions and circuits that are involved in anxiety disorders. When a threat is perceived, the senses dispatch signals to two different parts of the brain. One signal is directed to the cerebral cortex, the thinking part of the brain, but it takes a circuitous route. The other signal heads straight for the amygdala, a small, almond-shaped structure deep inside the brain. There it sets off a very rapid, automatic response that mobilizes the brain and body to deal with the danger at hand. This amygdala-based fear response swings into action before the thinking part of the brain is even aware of what's happening. Interestingly, researchers have found that the amygdala can be activated not only by danger, but also by the unexpected.

Once the amygdala's rapid-response system has been activated, stress hormones are released into the blood. The heart beats faster, and blood is diverted from internal organs to the muscles, where it may be needed for quick action. Meanwhile, glucose pours into the bloodstream, where it supplies the energy necessary for fighting or fleeing. To protect the person in future confrontations with the same threat, a blueprint of the learned fear response is etched onto the amygdala.

In the face of real danger, the fear response serves a protective function, and in a dire emergency, it can be a literal life-

> In the face of real danger, the fear response serves a protective function, and in a dire emergency, it can be a literal lifesaver.

saver. The problem arises when frightening or unexpected events prime a person's brain to overreact to relatively harmless situations. It's easy to see how the learned fear response that is etched onto the brain might be a hindrance rather than a help in such cases. But how could this one process give rise to several different types of dysfunctional fear and anxiety? Scientists are still investigating this question. Some research indicates that different anxiety disorders may be associated with activation in different parts of the amygdala.

While the amygdala is the first part of the brain activated, sensory information about the threat soon reaches the cerebral cortex as well. At this point, the person is able to rationally appraise the situation. As already noted, the goal of CBT is to improve the accuracy of such appraisals. Ultimately, the aim is to increase cognitive control over the person's fear response.

A Window into the Brain

New brain imaging technology allows scientists to peer inside the living brain and observe it at work. Below is a sampling of recent findings from imaging studies.

- GAD—In children with GAD, the volume of the amygdala tends to be larger, compared to children without the disorder.

- OCD—In adults, scientists have found abnormalities in a brain circuit involving the thalamus (a structure that acts as a relay station for incoming sensory information), basal ganglia (a cluster of neurons that play a key role in movement and behavior), and prefrontal cortex (the front part of the cerebral cortex). Similar abnormalities have been found in children and adolescents who have OCD.

- PTSD—The hippocampus (part of the brain involved in emotion, learning, and memory) tends to be smaller in adults with PTSD than in those without the disorder. However, children don't show this difference.

Neurotransmitters

On a chemical level, anxiety disorders may reflect imbalances in neurotransmitters. These are the messenger chemicals that nerve cells, called neurons, use to communicate with one another. Here's how it works: When a neuron is activated, an electrical signal travels from the cell body down a fiberlike branch, called the axon. Once it reaches the end of the axon, however, there's a challenge. A tiny gap, called a synapse, separates each neuron from its neighbor. That's where the neurotransmitter comes in. Its job is to chemically ferry the message across the gap.

There are many different kinds of neurotransmitters, each with a distinctive chemical shape. After a neurotransmitter has been released from the axon on the sending neuron, the communication process is still only half-complete. The neurotransmitter still must find a receptor molecule on the receiving neuron that has a matching shape. Think of the neurotransmitter as a key and the receptor as a lock. The message can only be delivered if the key fits the lock properly.

Think of the neurotransmitter as a key and the receptor as a lock.

When that happens, the receptor transmits the message into the receiving neuron, where it signals the cell to switch on or off. If the message is excitatory, it flips the switch on, and the neuron passes along the signal. If the message is inhibitory, it flips the switch off, and the neuron suppresses the signal. Either way, once the message has been delivered successfully, a feedback mechanism tells the sending neuron to stop pumping out new neurotransmitter. Now all that is left to do is dispose of the old neurotransmitter, which remains in the synapse. A molecule, called a transporter, is dispatched to bring it back across the gap to the axon that originally released it. There it is absorbed back into the sending neuron, a process called reuptake.

When it works, this is a remarkably complex and efficient system. However, like any complicated system, it occasionally breaks down. In some cases, receptors may be either too sensitive or not sensitive enough to a particular neurotransmitter. In other cases, the sending neuron may not release enough neurotransmitter, or it may reabsorb the chemical too soon, before it has delivered its message. Any of these communication failures can affect anxiety and mood.

Several neurotransmitters are thought to play a role in anxiety.

- Gamma-amino-butyric acid (GABA)—Inhibits the firing of neurons. GABA appears to help quell anxiety.
- Serotonin—Helps regulate mood, sleep, appetite, and sexual drive. Low levels of serotonin have been linked to both anxiety and depression.
- Norepinephrine—Helps regulate arousal, sleep, and blood pressure. Excess amounts of norepinephrine may trigger anxiety.
- Dopamine—Enables movement and influences motivation. Some evidence suggests that there may be a link between low dopamine and social anxiety disorder, and between excess dopamine and OCD.

Medications are believed to help correct and/or maintain the correct chemical balance in the brain to resolve the symptoms of anxiety. One common class of medications used to treat anxiety is the benzodiazepines, such as alprazolam (Xanax), diazepam (Valium), and lorazepam (Ativan). These drugs are thought to raise GABA levels within the brain. Another widely used class of the medications is the selective serotonin reuptake inhibitors (SSRIs), such as fluoxetine (Prozac), paroxetine (Paxil), and sertraline (Zoloft). These drugs slow the reuptake of serotonin, which increases the available supply of this neurotransmitter. Serotonin–norepinephrine reuptake inhibitors—including duloxetine (Cymbalta) and venlafaxine (Effexor)—affect serotonin much the way SSRIs do, but also affect norepinephrine. And buspirone (BuSpar), one of the first-studied antianxiety medications, increases serotonin activity while decreasing dopamine activity.

Hormones

While neurotransmitters carry messages within the brain, it is hormones that transport these messages via the bloodstream to tissues and organs throughout the rest of the body. Hormonal imbalances may affect anxiety, too. The most important hormones in this regard may be the ones involved in the body's response to threatening situations.

When a person perceives a threat, the amygdala isn't the only part of the brain that responds. The hypothalamus—part of the brain that serves as a command center for the body's hormonal and nervous systems—is activated as well. The hypothalamus releases a hormone called corticotropin-releasing factor (CRF). This hormone travels to the pituitary gland, located at the base of the brain, where it triggers the release of adrenocorticotropic hormone (ACTH). Then ACTH travels to the adrenal glands, located just above the kidneys, where it stimulates the release of a powerful stress hormone called cortisol. The rise in cortisol, in turn, stimulates a number of physiological effects, producing a burst of energy and alertness.

Taken together, these components make up a body system known as the hypothalamic–pituitary–adrenal axis. Some studies have found that people with anxiety disorders have imbalances in this system. The strongest association is seen between higher-than-average levels of CRF and PTSD. The excess CRF may explain why people with this disorder startle so easily.

It also may help explain why individuals who experience extreme stress or trauma early in life are at increased risk for developing an anxiety disorder as they get older. According to one theory, extreme stress early in childhood, when brain pathways are still developing, may affect the CRF-producing brain cells in a way that produces long-lasting overactivity. The lasting increase in CRF may lead to a super-sensitive response to even the slightest hint of threat.

Considerable evidence has now been amassed to support this theory. However, several key questions remain unanswered. For example, most of the studies supporting this theory have been done in animals or human adults. The findings in children have been less dramatic and sometimes contradictory, and the reasons for this discrepancy are still unclear. Also, not everyone who survives early trauma goes on to develop an anxiety disorder. This may be where a person's later life experiences, brain chemistry, and genetic makeup come into play. It appears that anxiety disorders represent the complex interaction of all these factors.

Autonomic Nervous System

The physiological response to fear involves not only hormones, but also the autonomic nervous system (ANS). This portion of the nervous system controls involuntary functions of internal organs. When the ANS is aroused, it produces effects such as rapid heartbeat, shortness of breath, and chest pain—in short, some of the classic symptoms associated with having a panic attack.

The association is especially marked among adults with panic attacks, in whom the autonomic nervous system tends to be overactive. Besides panic disorder, other conditions that may be related to autonomic overactivity include high blood pressure, heart disease, and a severe form of depression called melancholic depression.

Link Between Strep Throat and OCD

You can't catch an anxiety disorder the way you do a cold or the flu. However, there does seem to be a link between strep infections and a variant of childhood OCD called PANDAS (short for pediatric auto-immune neuropsychiatric disorders associated with streptococcal infections). PANDAS is characterized by a dramatic, "overnight" onset of OCD symptoms or tics. This sudden onset is usually pre-ceded by a case of strep throat. The mechanism behind PANDAS is not yet fully understood, but it seems that the body's immune re-sponse to the strep infection goes awry. In mounting an attack against invading bacteria, the immune system also mistakenly attacks the body's own tissues and cells. This is similar to what happens in rheumatic fever, another disorder that is triggered by strep. For more information about PANDAS, see Chapter 5.

The Genetics of Anxiety

At one time or another, all of us are confronted by stress, pres-sure, trauma, or tragedy. Yet not everyone develops an anxiety disorder. In many cases, genes may play a critical role in decid-ing who gets an anxiety disorder and who does not. Certain genetic variations may lead to chemical imbalances within the brain that predispose a person to anxiety. But this predisposi-tion may lie dormant until it is awakened by intense stress or trauma. Therefore, the actual onset of an anxiety disorder may de-pend on an interaction between genes and the environment.

People who have a parent or sibling with an anxiety disorder are at increased risk of developing one themselves.

People who have a parent or sibling with an anxiety disorder are at increased risk of developing one themselves. In part, this might be due to learning from anxious role models or growing up in the same stressful environment. However, twin and adoption studies show that heredity itself is also a factor. Researchers are currently working to pinpoint the precise genes involved. Although much remains to be learned, it seems that anxiety disorders are probably the result of many genes working in concert.

Specific Genes

So far, the best case has been made for an association between anxiety and a gene called 5-HTT. As a serotonin transporter gene, 5-HTT helps regulate the amount of serotonin that is present in the brain. A particular variation of this gene produces low levels of serotonin. Research has shown that the variation is more prevalent in people with GAD and OCD than in the general population.

One interesting study was published in the *Journal of Abnormal Psychology* in 2000. Seventy-two people with no history of panic attacks or anxiety disorders agreed to give blood samples, which were analyzed to see who had the 5-HTT variation. Each person then breathed a mixture of carbon dioxide and oxygen that causes temporary shortness of breath, a sensation sometimes associated with panic attacks. The test only provoked fear in the group with the genetic variation. Since none of the individuals in either group already had an anxiety disorder, it's obvious that the variation alone wasn't enough to cause anxiety. However, it seems that having the variation might set the stage for panicky feelings and perhaps a full-blown anxiety disorder if a stressful enough situation is encountered in the future.

Several other genes have been implicated in anxiety as well. These include genetic variations linked to panic disorder, agoraphobia, specific phobias, and social anxiety disorder. Researchers hope that a better understanding of how these genes interact with the environment will eventually lead to advances in treatment and prevention.

Temperament

The term "temperament" refers to individual differences in emotional reactivity that remain relatively stable over time as children grow up. Some basic differences in temperament are apparent from earliest infancy, which has led researchers to conclude that they are inherited. Individuals born with certain types of temperament may be predisposed to anxiety disorders later in life.

One way of classifying temperament involves comparing shy, timid children with their more outgoing, bold peers. According to psychologist Jerome Kagan, babies and children in the former group show a general pattern of inhibited behavior. Their first reaction to an unfamiliar situation tends to be avoidance, distress, or a subdued demeanor. By adolescence, the risk of social anxiety is higher in individuals who had been inhibited as toddlers than in those who were uninhibited. Researchers have also found a relationship between inhibited behavior and an overactive amygdala.

> By adolescence, the risk of social anxiety is higher in individuals who had been inhibited as toddlers than in those who were uninhibited.

Looking back, some parents say they recall seeing the first hints of anxiousness in their children long before the onset of a full-blown anxiety disorder. "She was always a fearful child," says one mother, who first noticed this trait when her daughter was still a toddler. Nevertheless, it's worth remembering that many shy, timid preschoolers don't grow up to have an anxiety disorder, while some outgoing, adventurous preschoolers do. Like all the other genetic, biological, and psychological factors, temperament is just one part of the total picture.

If You're Anxious, Too

Since anxiety can run in families, it's not uncommon for a teen with an anxiety disorder to have a parent with one of these disorders as well. Certainly, no one would wish for a family history of any illness. Yet many parents who find themselves in this situation say there is at least one advantage: If you've struggled with anxiety yourself, you may find it easier to understand what your teen is going through, because you've been there, too.

"What helped me first notice the OCD traits in my son was that I saw how much he acted like me," says Carl, who also has OCD. "When I was his age, I had nobody to talk to about it, and that felt really bad. I think it made me fall deeper and deeper into my own world." Carl was determined that things would be different for his son, so he made a concerted effort to keep the lines of communication open. He also sought professional help promptly for the 13-year-old, even though he did not begin his own treatment until after age 30. Says Carl, "I want to be the kind of parent who says, 'I'm smart about this. I know where to get help for my child

> "I want to be the kind of parent who says, 'I'm smart about this.'"

so he doesn't have to suffer the way I did for so many years.'"

If you're troubled by anxiety and haven't already sought help for it, take this opportunity to do so. By getting treatment and learning to manage your personal symptoms, you make yourself more emotionally available to your teen. As your own anxiety improves, you'll be better able to model the positive coping strategies you want your teen to learn. In addition, you'll be less likely to overreact to your teen's anxiety in a way that just fans the flames of fear and worry.

"Is It My Fault?"

Are you to blame for your teen's anxiety disorder? The short answer is no. Anxiety disorders are complex illnesses with multiple causes, many of which are rooted in biology and genetics. Certainly, the love and attention you give your teen have a powerfully positive influence. But children raised by loving, attentive, competent parents are not immune to anxiety disorders.

Unfortunately, "a lot of people still want to blame the parents," says the mother of two teenagers with OCD. "I've actually had people suggest that I could fix things by taking parenting classes. And my response was, 'If you're saying that there's a class on how to parent children with OCD, I'd be very interested in that. But if you're saying that this wouldn't have happened if I were a better parent, then you're misinformed.'" Then she offered to provide more information. Nothing shatters a stereotype like the facts.

Dangers of Doing Nothing

Reading a book about adolescent anxiety disorders is enough to make you feel—well, anxious. No parent likes to think that his or her child is in distress. It would be so easy to look the other way and deny the problem. Unfortunately, this "easy" solution may lead to more difficult problems down the road. Like other illnesses, anxiety disorders are only apt to get worse without proper treatment. They can also result in a number of complications; for example:

- School refusal—Extreme reluctance to go to school is sometimes seen in young people with separation anxiety, social anxiety disorder, and GAD. Unless dealt with promptly, it can have serious academic and social repercussions.

- Social isolation—Individuals with social anxiety disorder, agoraphobia, and other anxiety disorders may cut themselves off from other people. Unfortunately, this deprives them of much-needed emotional and practical support.
- Depression—Any tendency toward depression may be magnified by the avoidance of activities that might otherwise be fun and relaxing.
- Substance abuse—Some people with anxiety disorders turn to alcohol or other drugs in a misguided effort to relieve their emotional distress.
- Physical illnesses—Anxiety can be caused by or coexist with a number of physical illnesses, such as thyroid disorders, hypoglycemia, irritable bowel syndrome, pneumonia, and encephalitis. The course of the illness may be prolonged or worsened by the anxiety.

If left untreated, anxiety disorders are likely to interfere with everyday activities and strain relationships with friends and family. Anxiety can also lead to considerable distress or constant agonizing. These feelings, in turn, may distract adolescents from the vital business of learning. Meanwhile, avoidance behaviors may keep teens from fully participating in this special time in their lives. Just when teens should be spreading their wings, anxieties and fears can ground them.

Benefits of Getting Help

The good news is that it doesn't have to be this way. While there are no miracle cures, there *are* effective treatments that can significantly reduce the symptoms of anxiety. Research shows that CBT, which aims to correct ingrained patterns of thinking and behavior that may be contributing to a person's symptoms, is often especially helpful in this regard. Typically, systematic exposure to feared objects or situations is incorporated into the therapy. Medications may also be necessary as part of an adolescent's treatment plans.

No single treatment regimen is right for everyone. Instead, treatment needs to be individualized to a person's needs. Factors to be considered include the type of anxiety disorder, its severity, the primary symptoms, and the presence of coexisting conditions, such as depression or substance abuse. Some people respond to treatment in a matter of weeks or months, while others take a year or more. With time, however, the vast majority of teens with anxiety disorders can be helped to feel better. Once symptoms are under control, continued treatment can sometimes keep them from flaring up again or prevent another anxiety disorder from starting. In other cases, the symptoms can eventually return. But by knowing what to watch for, you and your teen can take effective action much more promptly.

Much of the rest of this book is devoted to providing the essential information you need to find proper treatment for your teen and support the recovery process at home. If you're new to this, it's important to know that things will indeed get better. "It was so painful watching what he went through, emotionally and socially and physically," says Luis's mother of his struggles with OCD and Tourette's. Today, though, Luis is a 17-year-old high school senior who aced his SAT and is looking forward to college. His mother says, "He's doing great. He understands the

"He's doing great. He understands the disorders, and he's happy and achieving in school."

disorders, and he's happy and achieving in school. We can look back now with such a sense of relief. Yet I know there are families out there who are where we were five or ten years ago. If I could talk to them, I would tell them that there's light at the end of the tunnel."

Chapter Three

Social Anxiety Disorder: Afraid of Embarrassment

What teenager hasn't stammered when called on unexpectedly in class, blushed when talking to a cute classmate, or felt the mortification of saying the wrong thing? The teenage years are rife with little embarrassments and small ego-bruisings, but most teens are able to pick themselves up, brush themselves off, and keep moving ahead. For those with social anxiety disorder, however, it's not that easy. Their anxiety about social situations may mushroom into a crippling fear of being judged or ridiculed. They may worry for days before a big social event, and they may spend hours afterward picking apart their every word and deed.

To understand what social anxiety disorder is, it's often helpful to think about what it *isn't*. It's not the shy, quiet disposition that comes naturally to some teens. It's not the case of nerves that most of us get from time to time before an important event. And it's not an imaginary condition that people can just wish away. Instead, it's a real illness with biological underpinnings, and it causes such intense fear in social situations that it can severely limit a person's life.

It's not an imaginary condition that people can just wish away.

Just because a teen has social anxiety doesn't necessarily mean he or she is socially inept. In fact, many people with the disorder are quite charming under the right circumstances. However, put them in a less familiar or comfortable situation, and they can become extremely anxious. Whether they're standing in front of a group or blending into a crowd, people experiencing social anxiety feel as if all eyes are on them. Their anxiety centers around the fear that they'll be judged harshly or do something to embarrass or humiliate themselves.

One Family's Story

Teens with social anxiety disorder may or may not be anxious about interacting with adults or younger children. But they do get anxious, at least some of the time, around other young people of their same age. "Katie had very few friends in her teens," says Suzanne of her daughter. "I had no idea why, because she could be really outgoing at times. I mean, if she was at a cocktail party with adults, she wouldn't have any problem at all. She was always good with younger children, too. It was just being around peers that she had trouble with."

For Suzanne, her daughter's lack of friends was as mystifying as it was worrisome. "At home or in a comfortable environment, she was truly the most creative and funny person you've ever met." Eventually, though, Suzanne recognized the depth of her daughter's anxiety. She realized that she was seeing a side of Katie that classmates never glimpsed. As Suzanne puts it, "If you're so anxious that you're not even talking, people aren't going to have a chance to get to know how great you are."

At first, Katie was reluctant to tackle the problem in therapy. Says Suzanne, "Her reasoning went something like this: 'Okay,

I'm 13 now, and I like being around 20-year-olds. So in a few years, I'll be 20, and everything will be all right.'" Not so, the therapist replied. She explained that, without treatment, Katie at 20 might only be comfortable with 40-year-olds, and Katie at 40 might be socializing with retirees. Eventually, Suzanne says, "Katie decided to reclaim her life."

Therapy helped substantially, but Katie still struggled to make friends throughout middle school and high school. Yet it was during these years that she also made an important discovery about herself. Says Suzanne, "The same girl who would throw up at the thought of going to a party was perfectly at home on a stage." Today, Katie is a 22-year-old theater major at a large university. She's enjoying not only her classes but, increasingly, her classmates as well. In fact, when Suzanne was interviewed for this book, her daughter was traveling on tour with a theater group. Says Suzanne, "For these other kids who are out of town, it's just about having a good time. But for Katie, it's a real emotional accomplishment."

> "For these other kids who are out of town, it's just about having a good time. But for Katie, it's a real emotional accomplishment."

Beyond Self-Consciousness

People such as Katie who suffer from social anxiety disorder are preoccupied with the fear that they'll embarrass themselves or be held up to ridicule. For some, the anxiety is limited to just a few, specific situations. For example, some people are petrified by the prospect of public speaking. They fear that listeners will notice their discomfort and judge them harshly as a result. Other people become very anxious about one-on-one conversation, fearing that their extreme self-consciousness will make them

Day-to-Day Fears

Social anxiety disorder can be debilitating when it leads people to avoid common, everyday experiences. While such experiences may seem mundane, they help teens learn how to function comfortably in society, so missing out on them may be no trivial loss. Commonplace triggers for social anxiety include:

- Speaking to a group of people
- Arriving after others are seated
- Being introduced to strangers
- Ordering in a restaurant
- Eating or drinking in public
- Returning items to a store
- Writing in front of people
- Using a public restroom

seem dull and boring. Still others avoid eating, drinking, or writing in public, fearing that their shaky hands will betray their anxiety to all around. Yet these same individuals may be totally at ease in other social situations.

Another group of people have generalized social anxiety, which means they feel fear in a wide range of social settings. For example, a particular teen might be afraid of talking in a group, engaging in one-on-one conversation, eating in front of other people, *and* going to parties. This generalized form of social anxiety disorder typically starts earlier and lasts longer than the more restricted type. It's also more likely to be associated with social skill deficits or severe problems at school.

Red Face, Clammy Hands

When people with social anxiety disorder find themselves in one of their trigger situations, they almost always respond with intense anxiety. Some symptoms—such as blushing, clammy hands, sweating, a shaky voice, or trembling—are apparent to others. Those with the disorder may be convinced that everyone notices their distress, and that no one else ever feels that way. Less visible symptoms include a racing heart, stomachaches, diarrhea, and tense, tight muscles. Occasionally, people with social anxiety even experience full-blown panic attacks.

Most adolescents and adults are acutely aware that their fear is excessive or irrational. Yet they feel unable to control it. As a result, many spend considerable time and energy avoiding the feared situation. Others endure it, but only at the expense of great trepidation and distress. Either way, the anxiety can consume more and more of their life, getting in the way of their activities and relationships.

As time goes on, a vicious cycle may be established. Dread leads to poor performance, which just increases the dread. Let's say a teen is afraid of speaking in public. An upcoming presentation in front of the class is enough to set off waves of worry for days and keep him awake for several nights. By the time the presentation finally arrives, the teen is so nervous that he winds up stammering and blushing. This bad experience just reinforces his worst fears. The next time he's called on to speak in class, he's even more nervous and afraid of embarrassing himself than before.

An upcoming presentation in front of the class is enough to set off waves of worry for days and keep him awake for several nights.

Red Flags to Watch For

Do you think your teen may be suffering from social anxiety disorder? These are some warning signs that your teen might need help:

- Excessive concern about being judged by people other than family members
- Nervous blushing, trembling, or sweating
- Confusion or freezing in social situations
- Trouble talking in class or reading aloud
- Discomfort with being the center of attention
- Unwillingness to invite friends to get together
- Hesitance to start conversations
- Reluctance to make phone calls
- Avoidance of eye contact with others
- Refusal to attend school or social events
- Speaking very softly or mumbling
- Hanging back during group activities

The complete diagnostic criteria for social anxiety disorder can be found in the Appendix.

Social Anxiety Disorder in Adolescents

As young people move from childhood to adolescence, it's very common for them to become preoccupied with social matters and worried about how they measure up against their friends. A little self-consciousness is to be expected. It's only when teens experience extreme or crippling social fears on a regular basis that they may have social anxiety disorder. Typically, the disorder starts in late childhood or early adolescence. Sometimes, it begins suddenly after an embarrassing incident. But other times, there's no obvious trigger, and the onset is gradual.

Although the precise number of people affected is unknown, it's estimated that from 3% to 13% of Americans may have social anxiety disorder at some point in their lives. The disorder seems to strike females about twice as often as males. However, a higher proportion of males seek help for it, so the number of people getting treatment for social anxiety disorder is roughly equal between the sexes.

Compared to their nonanxious peers, teens with social anxiety disorder are more likely to report having few friends, feeling lonely or depressed, and seeing themselves as socially incompetent. Carolanne says, "My 17-year-old daughter goes out every Friday and Saturday night and has loads of friends. But my 18-year-old [who is now a college freshman] never went on a date or to a party all through high school, even though she's a very pretty girl who the other kids thought was cool." While still in high school, Carolanne's older daughter created some artwork that was shown on network television and in a national magazine. Yet, despite having so much going for her, she missed out on the social life that is often the highlight of these years.

School Refusal

Typically, teens with social anxiety disorder go to school, but suffer in the process. Occasionally, though, they may resist going to school at all. Of course, middle school and high school students have been known to skip school for all kinds of reasons, many of which have nothing to do with anxiety. But when the problem is garden-variety truancy, teens typically try to hide their school absences from their parents.

In contrast, teens with social anxiety disorder may try to persuade their parents to allow them to miss school. Rather than getting into trouble, they usually just want to pass their days quietly at home. Many such teens are quite willing to do schoolwork. It's the social demands at school that they so desperately want to avoid. For such teens, getting treatment for the underlying anxiety usually helps the school issues as well.

Other Related Problems

Selective mutism is an uncommon condition in which children refuse to speak in certain social situations, such as at school. These children are physically and mentally capable of speaking, and they may even be quite talkative at home. However, they clam up completely in anxiety-provoking situations. Selective mutism usually begins before age 5, although it may not be diagnosed until children start school. Typically, children outgrow the condition before adolescence. However, it's possible that selective mutism might be a harbinger of things to come. Although the exact nature of selective mutism is still being debated in scientific circles, many experts believe that it may be a childhood form of social anxiety disorder.

Teens with social anxiety may sometimes turn to alcohol or other drugs in a misguided effort to relieve their misery. Research indicates that about 20% of adults with social anxiety disorder abuse alcohol. While for some, this may be a direct response to the disorder, for others, it may be tied to the depression that so often goes hand in hand with anxiety. Studies have found that about half of people with social anxiety disorder suffer from depression as well.

There is also some evidence that people with social anxiety disorder may be at risk for eating disorders. One large study published in the *American Journal of Psychiatry* in 2004 found that about 20% of individuals with an eating disorder had also experienced social anxiety disorder at some point in their lives. This held true for both anorexia nervosa and bulimia nervosa. Anorexia nervosa is an eating disorder in which people have an intense fear of becoming fat, so they severely restrict what they eat, often to the point of near starvation. Bulimia nervosa is an eating disorder in which people binge on large quantities of food, then purge by forced vomiting, laxative or diuretic abuse, or excessive exercise.

The basis for the connection between social anxiety and eating disorders is still being studied. Often, however, the anxiety seems to come first. Some researchers have suggested that an excessive concern about being judged might set the stage for an unhealthy preoccupation with body weight.

> *The basis for the connection between social anxiety and eating disorders is still being studied.*

Causes and Contributors

Like other anxiety disorders, social anxiety seems to have multiple causes, including both heredity and the environment. Twin studies have found strong evidence for a link between genes and social anxiety disorder. However, genes alone can't explain why things go awry. Life experiences also seem to be important contributing factors.

Shy by Nature

One way in which genes may influence social anxiety is through innate temperament. Some children just seem shyer and more timid than their peers from the day they're born. Psychologist Jerome Kagan and his colleagues have referred to these youngsters as behaviorally inhibited. As babies, these children may cry frequently. As toddlers, they may be shy and fearful. And by the time they're school age, many tend to be rather socially withdrawn. As one mother recalls, "Even when my daughter was little, I realized that socializing was a problem. I tried to help by setting up play days in families where the children weren't too assertive, which scared my daughter, and where the moms were kind and understanding."

Not all such youngsters grow up to develop full-fledged social anxiety disorder. But as you might expect, a considerable number do. The risk of social anxiety disorder in adolescents who were behaviorally inhibited as young children is significantly higher than in adolescents who were less inhibited. Nevertheless, many shy, quiet toddlers never go on to develop social anxiety disorder, while some of their outgoing, boisterous peers do. Clearly, temperament isn't the only thing that matters.

Environmental Factors

Research has shown that stressful life events—for example, being physically or sexually abused, failing a grade, dropping out of school, getting into trouble with the law, being placed in the child welfare system, or having parents who are separated or divorced—can raise the risk of social anxiety disorder. The more such factors teens have in their lives, the greater the risk seems to be.

Parents are an important influence, too. Research suggests that social fears may be learned, at least in part, by observing others. If parents act shy, fearful, or withdrawn, their children may imitate this behavior. In addition, some parents may unintentionally reward fearful behavior in their children by smothering them with attention when they act afraid. Other parents may contribute to their children's anxiety by being either overly protective or overly judgmental.

If parents act shy, fearful, or withdrawn, their children may imitate this behavior.

However, it's worth remembering that family relationships are a two-way street. Children who are very socially anxious may naturally bring out more protectiveness in their parents. This encourages the children to become more timid and withdrawn, which only elicits more protectiveness, and so on. Soon, a self-defeating cycle may be established in which young people never get an opportunity to learn ways to manage their own anxiety. In such cases, it's not that the parents *caused* the anxiety but rather that they unwittingly helped perpetuate it.

Classmates and acquaintances figure into the equation as well. Teens who are very fearful about making social contact tend to distance themselves from others and have few friends. To outsiders, this behavior can look strange or aloof. As a result, the anxious teens may indeed wind up being ridiculed or rejected. Their worst fears confirmed, they may grow even more anxious. The very thing they sought to avoid becomes a self-fulfilling prophesy.

Physiological Factors

As with all anxiety disorders, there is also a physiological component to social anxiety. The amygdala, the small structure inside the brain that controls fear responses, is believed to play a key role. In brain imaging studies, adults with social anxiety disorder who were shown pictures of faces or asked to speak in front of an audience showed greater activity in the amygdala than their nonanxious counterparts. They also had an unusual pattern of activity in other parts of the brain that make up a specialized system for evaluating social cues and deciding whether a threat is present. Researchers believe that this system may be overactive in people with social anxiety, leading the brain to send out a "threat!" alarm even in harmless situations.

Medications for social anxiety disorder change the way the brain works by affecting levels of key neurotransmitters, the chemical messengers within the brain. But what many people don't realize is that learning, such as the learning that occurs in therapy, affects the brain as well. One interesting study from Uppsala University in Sweden looked at the responses of adults with social anxiety disorder who were treated with either medication or cognitive-behavioral therapy (CBT). After nine weeks, both treatment groups had improved about the same extent, while a third group that was merely put on a waiting list had gotten no better. In brain scans, both treatment groups also showed similar decreases in brain activity during public speaking. The decreases were seen in the amygdala, the hippocampus (part of the brain involved in emotion, learning, and memory), and several adjoining areas. As this study clearly demonstrated, both medications and therapy can attack the physiological roots of social anxiety.

Diagnosis and Treatment

Understanding the source of social anxiety is one thing. Coping with it in daily life can be quite another. As a parent, watching your teen struggle with fears and insecurities can be a heartwrenching experience. Knowing when and where to reach out for help can make all the difference—not only for your teen's well-being, but also for your own peace of mind.

As a parent, watching your teen struggle with fears and insecurities can be a heartwrenching experience.

Getting a Diagnosis

The first step is to find out what you're really up against. Some pediatricians are familiar enough with social anxiety disorder to recognize it when they see it, but others are not. If you think your teen may be suffering from an anxiety disorder, ask your doctor for a referral to a mental health professional. Ideally, this should be someone who specializes in anxiety disorders and has substantial experience with young people. Other possible sources for referrals include teachers, clergy, and support groups, such as the Anxiety Disorders Association of America.

To make a diagnosis, the mental health professional will talk with you and your teen and observe your teen's behavior. No one knows your child better than you do, so you'll be asked to supply information about your teen's past history and current symptoms. Since adolescence is a time of rapid change that brings with it a steady stream of new challenges, it's not always easy to tell the difference between normal bumps in the developmental path and more serious detours. To sort out the difference, the professional will look for symptoms that meet the criteria for social anxiety disorder and cause substantial distress or disrupt the teen's life.

The professional will also look for signs that the teen is having trouble bouncing back from everyday stresses and strains. There's nothing at all unusual about a teenager whose heart pounds and palms get clammy around an attractive classmate. What's more unusual—and perhaps a tip-off to social anxiety disorder—is if the teen frets about the incident for days afterward or becomes so worried about it happening again that he or she begins to skip class.

If you think your teen may have social anxiety disorder, now is the time to seek help. Studies indicate that a large majority of people who receive treatment for the disorder feel better afterward and say they're able to get their social anxiety under control. The main treatment options are CBT, medication, or a combination of the two.

Cognitive-Behavioral Therapy

CBT is the leading form of therapy for social anxiety disorder. It helps people recognize and change self-defeating thought patterns as well as identify and change maladaptive behaviors.

Three randomized controlled clinical trials—the gold standard in clinical research—have now shown that CBT is an effective treatment for social anxiety in adolescents.

To understand the role that thoughts and behavior play in social anxiety disorder, consider this example: Let's say a teen is convinced that other people will think everything she says is stupid or boring. When she's called on in class, even though she knows the material well, the first thought that automatically pops into her mind is, "Oh no, I'm going to blow it." This sets off a chain reaction of other thoughts, such as "They'll think I'm an idiot" and "Everybody's going to laugh at me." Such irrationally negative thinking leads to an increase in self-focused attention. This, in turn, can lead to behavior such as forgetting the answer or mumbling it incoherently. Together, the thinking and the behavior conspire to ensure that this teen's initial fears are realized.

At home that night, the teen may rerun the scene in her mind a hundred times, each time mentally chastising herself for her "stupidity." The following morning, she feels queasy just thinking about going to class. Her anxiety is spiraling out of control, guaranteeing that she'll be even more nervous and less able to respond appropriately the next time she's called on.

At home that night, the teen may rerun the scene in her mind a hundred times, each time mentally chastising herself for her "stupidity."

CBT attempts to break this chain of thoughts and behaviors. The cognitive part of treatment starts by having a person take note of his or her thoughts and anxiety levels in various settings. Later, the therapist and patient discuss the thoughts and evaluate how realistic they are, given the facts of the situation. The patient may be challenged to test his or her beliefs or consider whether the worst-case outcome would really be all that disastrous. Finally, the therapist and patient work together to replace unrealistic thoughts with more realistic ones.

CBT can also include teaching the patient specific skills that help reduce stress and give the person a greater sense of control in difficult situations. For example, the patient may learn deep breathing techniques that relax the body and reverse some of the physiological changes brought on by stress. Or the patient may be coached in specific social skills, such as how to maintain eye contact or carry on a conversation.

Exposure Therapy

One particular form of CBT that has proved to be especially useful for treating anxiety is exposure therapy, in which people are systematically exposed to the situations that frighten them. The underlying premise is that the best way to overcome a fear is by facing it head-on. This type of therapy seems to be especially valuable in the treatment of social anxiety disorder.

Exposure therapy can be done in several ways. Patients may be asked to imagine themselves in certain social situations, or they may role-play these scenarios during therapy. Patients may also be given homework, in which they're asked to put themselves in real-life social situations that spark anxiety. Rather than jumping into a situation all at once, though, they're introduced to it in a stepwise fashion. The idea is to start with tasks that involve little risk of rejection or disapproval. The patients then gradually move on to higher-stakes tasks, but only after they've built the self-confidence to handle any rejection or disapproval they might encounter. As positive social experiences mount, the fear and anxiety start to fade away.

Therapy for social anxiety disorder can be conducted either one-on-one with a cognitive-behavioral therapist or in a small

---

1-2-3-Contact!

When it comes to helping your teen make social contact, it's one step at a time. Suzanne says a cognitive-behavioral therapist helped her daughter devise a plan for making friends as part of her exposure therapy. "First, Katie called up a classmate to ask about homework," says Suzanne. "Then she called a classmate and talked for a few minutes. Finally, she made limited, organized social plans, such as going to a movie." At that point, open-ended "hanging out" still made Katie very anxious. But following a step-by-step plan had helped her gradually reduce her fear and increase her self-confidence.

---

group that is led by a therapist and made up of people with similar anxiety problems. Group therapy gives teens a chance to try out their new social skills in a safe environment before venturing into riskier situations. Group members also benefit by observing how others cope.

Medication Therapy

A number of medications have also proved to be useful for people with social anxiety disorder. In studies, about 70% of adults who take medication for social anxiety disorder improve, compared to just 30% of those who receive a placebo (sugar pill). Few studies have looked at medication therapy in children or adolescents with the disorder, and more research is sorely needed in this area. Nevertheless, doctors prescribe medications for young people based on clinical experience and the results of studies in adults. The medications generally fall into one of three classes: selective serotonin

Doctors prescribe medications for young people based on clinical experience and the results of studies in adults.

reuptake inhibitors (SSRIs), serotonin–norepinephrine reuptake inhibitors (SNRIs), and benzodiazepines.

- SSRIs—These medications are classified as antidepressants, but they're also widely used to treat anxiety disorders. They act by increasing the available supply of serotonin, a key neurotransmitter in the brain. SSRIs include citalopram (Celexa), escitalopram (Lexapro), fluoxetine (Prozac), fluvoxamine (Luvox), paroxetine (Paxil), and sertraline (Zoloft). One study of fluvoxamine in young people ages 6 to 17 found that it was an effective treatment for social anxiety disorder. In adults, studies have shown the benefits of fluvoxamine, paroxetine, and sertraline for those with generalized social anxiety. It can take a few weeks for the full effects of SSRIs to be felt. Possible side effects include nausea, headache, nervousness, insomnia, jitteriness, and sexual problems. In 2004, the U.S. Food and Drug Administration (FDA) also issued a warning about a small but significant risk of increased suicidal thoughts and behaviors in children and adolescents who are taking antidepressants. For more information about this warning, see Chapter 7.
- SNRIs—Two newer antidepressants—duloxetine (Cymbalta) and venlafaxine (Effexor)—act on serotonin much like SSRIs do, but also affect another neurotransmitter called norepinephrine. These medications are sometimes prescribed for anxiety as well as depression. Research in adults has shown that venlafaxine is effective for generalized social anxiety. It can take a few weeks to get the full benefits of these drugs. The side effects are similar to those for SSRIs, and the FDA warning about the risk of suicidal thoughts and behaviors applies here as well.

- Benzodiazepines—These antianxiety medications are thought to raise levels of gamma-amino-butyric acid, yet another neurotransmitter that seems to play a role in anxiety. Benzodiazepines include alprazolam (Xanax), chlordiazepoxide (Librium), clonazepam (Klonopin), clorazepate (Tranxene), diazepam (Valium), lorazepam (Ativan), and oxazepam (Serax). One advantage to these drugs is that they are fast-acting. Some people who take them feel better from the very first day. Possible side effects include drowsiness, loss of coordination, fatigue, confusion, or mental slowing. If your teen is old enough to drive, he or she may be advised not to do so while taking one of these medications. If your teen has a substance abuse problem, be aware that combining these drugs with alcohol can lead to serious or even life-threatening complications. Also, benzodiazepines themselves can be abused, so their use needs to be closely supervised. For more information about the side effects of antianxiety drugs, see Chapter 7.

Of all these medications, only paroxetine (Paxil), sertraline (Zoloft), and venlafaxine (Effexor) have been specifically approved by the FDA for the treatment of social anxiety disorder, and those three drugs have been approved only for use in adults. Nevertheless, once a drug has FDA approval for any indication, doctors are allowed to prescribe it for other purposes and age groups based on their clinical judgment. The use of medications to treat social anxiety disorder in adolescents is becoming increasingly common.

The use of medications to treat social anxiety disorder in adolescents is becoming increasingly common.

Rx for Performance Anxiety

Performance anxiety is a limited form of social anxiety in which the excessive fear relates to performing a specific task in front of others. Examples include stage fright or test anxiety. Beta-blockers—medications such as propranolol (Inderal) that are usually prescribed for high blood pressure or heart problems—are sometimes used to treat performance anxiety as well. They slow the heart rate and reduce sweating and trembling. By decreasing the physiological signs of fear, they may help a person feel less anxious or panicky long enough to get through a big performance or test. However, beta-blockers don't seem to be useful for treating more generalized social anxiety.

The Best Treatment

What's the best treatment approach for *your* teen? The answer varies depending on a number of factors, including the nature and severity of your teen's symptoms, the presence of other problems, and your teen's lifestyle and preferences. In general, CBT with exposure therapy has some advantages over medication. It has been better tested in adolescents, and it doesn't carry the same risk of side effects. Studies in adults suggest that at least half of people with social anxiety disorder improve with therapy, and the improvement is sometimes quite dramatic. In addition, people learn skills in CBT that they can apply for the rest of their lives.

On the other hand, exposure therapy is arguably the most important part of CBT for social anxiety disorder, and therapists with experience and training in exposure therapy are hard to find in many parts of the country. Exposure therapy also requires that your teen be willing to play an active role in treatment. In the course of therapy, your teen will be called upon to confront frightening situations and endure a short-term increase in fear and anxiety in order to achieve long-term goals. Some teens simply aren't ready to make that commitment.

For teens who aren't willing or able to participate in therapy or when cognitive-behavioral therapy does not work, medication offers another valuable option. For those who don't get adequate relief from either therapy or medication alone, a combination of both may be tried. In fact, some treatment providers recommend combination therapy right from the start, on the assumption that both treatments together are stronger than either alone. While that seems logical, no studies have yet tested whether combination therapy really does produce superior results in young people with social anxiety.

When weighing treatment options, make sure both you and your teen understand the benefits and risks of each and what will be expected of you. If you have questions or concerns, don't hesitate to speak up. A good therapist or doctor should welcome the dialogue. "My child's therapist was wonderful," says one mother. "She laid out exactly what she was going to do for the social anxiety. She explained what the problem was, what the result would be if we didn't do anything, what the treatment path was, and how long it was expected to take."

Supporting Your Teen at Home

Finding professional help for your teen is a major step, but your role doesn't end there. You make a tremendous difference in your teen's life by all the things you do every day to show your love and support. While you're not responsible for your teen's anxiety, you *can* influence it in a positive way.

Three Traps to Avoid

Even parents with the best of intentions sometimes feed their children's anxiety without realizing it. These are three common errors that well-meaning parents often make.

- Being an anxious role model. If you have social anxiety yourself, you may believe it doesn't matter. After all, you might think, you don't have to be self-assured to encourage your teen to be that way. But your teen may do as you do, rather than as you say. If your own social anxiety isn't under control, you probably avoid social situations, have trouble meeting people, or feel awkward trying to carry on a conversation. Your teen might be picking up some of these behaviors from you by imitation. Fortunately, you can turn this situation around by getting help for your own anxiety. That way, you'll be modeling not only better coping strategies and social skills but also the ability to take charge of your life and make positive changes.

- Reacting critically to your teen's fears. Maybe you're normally an understanding person, but your teen's social anxiety just seems to set you off. You want to feel compassion, but instead you wind up feeling anger or disgust. One possibility is that your teen's anxiety may be an uncomfortable reminder of part of yourself that you'd rather deny. If that's the case, finding ways to build your own social confidence may help you not only feel happier with yourself, but also be more accepting toward your teen. If you're not sure where to start, a therapist or counselor may be able to point you in the right direction.

- Becoming overprotective. Perhaps you go to the other extreme. You jump in to "rescue" your teen at the slightest hint of anxiety or distress. Your intention is to protect your teen, but what you're actually doing is depriving your child of opportunities to face his or her fears. Remind yourself that confronting fears is a vital part of mastering them. Step back a few

Remind yourself that confronting fears is a vital part of mastering them.

Self-Help Strategies

Set a good example by using these self-help strategies for coping with social situations. Then encourage your teen to try them, too.

- Expose yourself to new social situations. For example, sign up for a fun activity or volunteer to work for a cause you care about.
- Prepare some conversation starters in advance. For example, you might read the newspaper to find interesting stories to talk about.
- Ask others about their hobbies and activities. This communicates your interest while providing a ready-made topic of conversation.
- Invite some neighbors over for dinner. This provides an extended opportunity to socialize and model conversation for your children.

paces, and allow your teen to take some social risks. You're not being uncaring. Quite the contrary, you're giving your teen room to learn and grow.

More Confidence Boosters

When your teen does tackle a new social challenge, let him or her know how much you admire the effort. As Sondra says, "When my daughter does something like going out with her friends, I try to reinforce it by being positive and proud of her. I say things like, 'Aren't you glad you did that? It was fun, right?'" In your teen's mind, his or her social failures may be magnified far out of proportion, while successes are easily overlooked. By pointing out the positives, you help your teen develop a more accurate self-image.

Teens with social anxiety disorder tend to not only underestimate their own social skills, but also overestimate the social ease of everyone else. Help your teen develop a more empathic view of others as well. For instance, if a new family with a teenage daughter moves into the neighborhood, you might say, "I'll bet she's feeling a little lost and out of place. Maybe you could introduce yourself while you're waiting for the school bus. She would probably feel a lot better knowing at least one person's name."

Encourage your teen to speak up for him or herself; for example, when ordering in a restaurant or asking for directions. If you're shopping for a new pair of sneakers, let your teen ask the salesclerk for help. If you're having trouble with the video game system, have your teen call the customer support line. Talking to a classmate about an assignment is a good way to practice chatting with peers. One mother says her teen's assignment from her cognitive-behavioral therapist was to call three people and ask them for the homework assignment, whether she needed it or not.

Help your teen work up to bigger goals gradually, starting with less demanding tasks and then slowly increasing the difficulty level. For example, let's say your teen's ultimate goal is to give a presentation in history class. He or she might first try talking to a few students outside class, then making a few comments in class, then participating in the presentation of a group project. By this point, your teen is better prepared to meet the challenge of giving a speech on his or her own.

Working with Your Teen's Teacher

It's no accident that most of the examples in this chapter deal with school situations. School is the site of many of your teen's most important social interactions. Consequently, it's also likely to be the focus of much of your teen's anxiety. Social anxiety can affect everything from speaking in class and taking tests to eating lunch in the cafeteria and participating in extracurricular activities. The more you can help your teen overcome school anxiety, the better your teen is apt to do in all these settings.

Make allies of your teen's teachers, the school counselor or psychologist, and other key school personnel. Working together, you can create an action plan that is individualized to meet your teen's needs. For example, if your teen is afraid of speaking in class, you or the teacher can:

> Make allies of your teen's teachers, the school counselor or psychologist, and other key school personnel.

- Explain that public speaking gets easier with practice.
- Look for ways to involve everyone in group activities.
- Gently prompt the student to join in class discussions.
- Praise the student for speaking up, but do so privately so that you don't embarrass the teen by making him or her the center of attention.
- Avoid punishing or shaming the student for not speaking.
- Include formal training in public speaking as part of the classroom curriculum. This is beneficial for everyone, and it lets those with social anxiety see that many of their classmates also find public speaking daunting.

Coping with School Refusal

In some cases, students with social anxiety disorder may resist going to a particular class or refuse to attend school at all. This is a challenging problem that needs to be addressed immediately, before your teen falls too far behind in schoolwork. Try

Dealing with Test Anxiety

Test anxiety can have different causes, but it often arises from performance anxiety about taking a test in class or being judged by the
teacher. If your teen has severe test anxiety, talk to the teacher about
possible accommodations. Explain that these strategies aren't meant
to give your teen an unfair advantage. They just help your teen perform up to his or her ability. This success, in turn, helps your teen
gradually gain the self-confidence to succeed in more demanding
test situations. Possible accommodations include:

- Letting the student take the test in private
- Allowing extra time to reduce pressure
- Focusing on correct answers rather than errors
- Conducting ungraded assessments
- Accepting portfolios in lieu of tests
- Teaching study skills and test-taking strategies

to get to the root cause. In some cases, your teen may have a
very reasonable concern, such as anxiety about a bully who is
harassing him or her between classes. In other cases, the core
concern may be more general, such as anxiety about looking
foolish or not fitting in. If your teen has trouble opening up to
you, suggest talking to a trusted teacher or the school counselor or psychologist.

Common concerns that may contribute to school refusal in
middle school and high school students include fear of:

- Being called on in class
- Eating in the cafeteria
- Using the school restroom
- Changing for gym class
- Riding on the school bus
- Being picked on by bullies

Once you've pinpointed the problem, you can start to look for solutions. One "solution" to avoid, however, is letting your teen stay home from school, no matter how much he or she may want to do so. Staying home just makes the school anxiety stronger and more stubbornly resistant to change. Instead, look for ways to reduce anxiety in the problem situation. If you don't see progress soon, consider

Staying home just makes the school anxiety stronger and more stubbornly resistant to change.

seeking professional help. A cognitive-behavioral therapist can help your teen devise a systematic plan for confronting and overcoming specific school fears.

Kim's Success Story

Kim's story illustrates the difference an involved parent and caring teachers can make. "Kim really struggled with social anxiety during her first year of high school, even though she attends a very tiny school of just 45 students," says her mother, Mary. Kim's grades suffered as a result. Over the past year, though, a combination of medication and family support helped her gain better control over her fears. As a tenth-grader, Kim has blossomed socially, and that has translated into better academic performance. Says Mary, "Now she regularly speaks up in class and even asked to read aloud in English. Her grades have improved to match her self-esteem. They're up by an average of 25%."

Mary worked closely with the teachers at Kim's small private school to help make these gains a reality. "Behind the scenes, I asked the teachers to partner her with other quiet students, eventually leading up to the more boisterous ones," Mary says. "And I asked that her locker be located between two kind students." Meanwhile, the teachers made a point of regularly calling on Kim in class and rewarding her when she spoke up. "My advice to parents is to remember that they're consumers and advocates," says Mary. "They know their children better than anyone. It's up to them to stand up for the right of their children to participate in society and to help them achieve their goals."

Looking to the Future

Not long ago, social anxiety disorder was considered a minor problem that young people would simply outgrow. In recent years, though, we've come to realize that severe social anxiety can have serious implications for academic and later occupational success. It can disrupt relationships and cause a tremendous amount of fear and worry. In addition, it can sap much of the enjoyment from life. As one parent puts it, "It was very sad and frustrating to see those years slip away without much of the fun that might have existed if she'd gotten help sooner."

The right treatment, coupled with support from caring family and friends, can greatly improve a teen's quality of life. It can open doors that social anxiety might otherwise keep closed—everything from making new friends to trying out for a sports team to applying to an out-of-state college. Even with the best results, however, the symptoms of social anxiety disorder may increase again if a new source of stress occurs. For example, a middle school student who seems to have conquered his social anxiety may be struck with a new bout of anxiety and insecurity upon starting high school. This time, though, the teen will be prepared. He'll know what to do and where to turn for help if the need arises.

Sadly, many people with social anxiety disorder believe they have no choice but to suffer in silence. You know differently, and that's a critical bit of knowledge you can pass on to your child.

> The symptoms of social anxiety disorder may increase again if a new source of stress occurs.

Chapter Four

Generalized Anxiety Disorder: Worried About Everything

What do adolescents have to worry about, anyway? They don't have full-time jobs or mortgages or bills, and they certainly don't have the responsibility of raising a teenager. Yet it turns out that adolescents, like adults, have plenty of things weighing on their minds—everything from grades and pimples to gangs and drugs to war and terrorism.

Indeed, teens today face so many stresses and pressures that a little worrying now and then is perfectly normal and realistic. It's only when the worry grabs hold of a teen's mind and won't let go that there may be a serious problem. The hallmark of generalized anxiety disorder (GAD) is exaggerated worry and tension that are unfounded or out of proportion to the situation. Teens with GAD always expect the worst. They worry about all kinds of things—schoolwork, appearance, money, friends, health, the future, and their performance in a wide range of situations, to name just a few common concerns. This state of constant, gnawing worry

The hallmark of generalized anxiety disorder (GAD) is exaggerated worry and tension that are unfounded or out of proportion to the situation.

lasts for months or even years. After a while, it can start to take a harsh toll on a teen's mental and physical health.

While it might be tempting to conclude that the teen just has a worrywart personality, there's more going on than that. GAD, like other anxiety disorders, is a disease with biological underpinnings. If left untreated, it can cause substantial hardship and suffering. This fact was highlighted in a 2004 survey by the Anxiety Disorders Association of America. The survey included more than 1,000 adults from across the United States, about half of whom had GAD. The majority of GAD sufferers indicated that their illness had a major impact on their relationships with significant others, friends, children, and coworkers. Most also said that GAD got in the way of their ability to go about their everyday activities.

Your teen has one big advantage over these grown-ups: a parent who is watching over the situation and eager to help. If treatment is needed, getting it early may save your teen from endless hours of worry. It may also improve the outlook for the future, by helping your teen become more attuned to anxiety and giving him or her tools for handling it more effectively.

One Family's Story

Kevin is a case in point. Anxiety seems to run in his family. His two siblings have both been diagnosed with obsessive-compulsive disorder (OCD), and his mother, Brenda, had a bout of agoraphobia when she was 21. Kevin, too, always seemed a bit more anxious than his friends. However, it didn't become a big problem until he turned 15. That's when he began worrying constantly about his health. Says Brenda, "He was always checking his heartbeat to make sure everything was okay."

Kevin worried about many other things as well. In fact, he seemed to live in a state of free-floating anxiety. "It waxed and waned," says Brenda. "Changes in his environment would exacerbate his symptoms." A change as small as going back to school after winter break would be enough to set the downward spiral in motion.

Eventually, though, Kevin grew better at recognizing when his worrying was getting out of hand. This gave him a chance to use the anxiety management skills he had learned from his mother, who happens to be a psychotherapist, and his sister, who was already in treatment for OCD. "Instead of adding more fear on top of the anxiety, he learned to sort of accept it, and then it would fade away," Brenda says. Kevin also took medication, and his mother says this made "a huge difference," too.

Today, Kevin is a 22-year-old journalism major at a large university. Now that he's a young adult, "he handles the anxiety much better," says Brenda. "Not that he doesn't still suffer at times. The anxiety still comes and goes, but he's not as upset by it. I really don't hear much about it anymore."

Ultimate Worrywarts

Brenda was especially tuned in to her son's anxiety because of her personal experience and professional training. But for those who aren't as savvy about anxiety disorders, GAD can be deceptive. It's easy to discount what those with the disorder are going through. After all, everyone worries from time to time, and GAD sufferers may not look that different from other folks on the outside. Inside, though, people with GAD may be tormented by constant worry to the point where they're always miserable. Their minds may be so preoccupied with worst-case scenarios that they have trouble concentrating on anything else. Their bodies may be so riddled with nonstop tension that it's nearly impossible for them to relax or get a restful night's sleep.

Teens with GAD may realize that they're worriers, but they feel unable to control the troubling thoughts. They may worry about big things, little things, or nothing in particular. Of course, people with other anxiety disorders tend to worry a lot as well, but the focus of their anxiety is more stable and specific. With GAD, the focus changes. It's the incessant fretting that always stays the same.

GAD affects the body as well as the mind. Young people with the disorder may suffer from frequent aches and pains or stomach upsets for which no other medical cause can be found. Marilyn says the first thing that tipped her off to her daughter's anxiety was the difference in the way she was breathing. "She started taking a ton of deep breaths, and I noticed it more when she was nervous," says Marilyn. "Then she developed a facial tic, and the more nervous she was, the worse it would be, too." When the pediatrician couldn't find any explanation for the problems, Marilyn took her daughter to a child psychiatrist, who diagnosed GAD.

Such teens may also be perfectionists who arrive on time, budget their allowances, and redo school assignments until everything is just so.

The Little Adult

Some young people with GAD seem old beyond their years because they're so preoccupied with schedules, finances, and health—concerns more typical of people their parent's age. Such teens may also be perfectionists who arrive on time, budget their allowances, and

Causes for Concern

Adolescents with GAD and other anxiety disorders have a world of things to worry about. This is just a small sampling of the worries that parents interviewed for this book said their children had shared. Some of these concerns might be indicative of other anxiety disorders if taken by themselves. It's only when people are chronically worried about all kinds of things that GAD is diagnosed.

- Being alone in the dark—Gloria says that her 13-year-old daughter gets especially anxious at night. "She'll plead, 'Momma, come lie down with me for a few minutes before I go to sleep.'" While this kind of bedtime routine might be common in young children, it's a warning sign when a teenager still needs this much reassurance at night.

- Being sick or hurt—Gloria's daughter also becomes very alarmed about her physical health. Once, she tripped and fell into the rounded corner of a dresser. "It wasn't a hard fall," says Gloria. "But she slid to the floor and cried, 'My legs don't work!'" Fortunately, it turned out that no real damage had been done. The overreaction was attributed to anxiety.

- Taking tests—Marilyn says that her 12-year-old daughter gets tied up in knots before tests, despite being a good student who's taking honors classes. "She has gotten three 100s in a row in social studies, and she's more than ready for the next test, because she has been studying a lot at home. Being prepared helps, but it doesn't totally get rid of her anxiety."

redo school assignments until everything is just so. These traits have their upside, of course, but they can be taken to an extreme. The self-imposed pressure may lead to occasional blow-ups, especially when there are unexpected changes in plans. Frequently, though, the deep distress of these teens goes quietly unnoticed. Parents may view their son or daughter as "the perfect child," without realizing how much turmoil lies beneath the punctual, organized facade.

One girl who fit this profile was a straight-A student who was taking advanced classes in high school. "She would literally throw up the night before any kind of school paper or presentation or test," says her mother. "My husband and I are the kind of parents who would say to her, 'So what if you make some mistakes? Big deal.'" But their daughter still wasn't willing to accept anything less than perfection from herself.

Teens with GAD may be quite anxious about how they measure up socially, academically, and athletically. Unlike young people with social anxiety disorder, however, those with GAD feel this way even when they aren't worried about being judged by others. They are their own harshest critics. Some try to allay their anxiety by seeking out constant feedback about how they're doing. It can reach the point where they have trouble getting anything done, because they spend so much time seeking out reassurance.

Red Flags to Watch For

Do you think your teen may be suffering from GAD? These are some warning signs that your teen might need help:

- Worrying about all sorts of events and activities
- Being keyed up or on edge all the time
- Getting tired more easily than he or she once did
- Seeming distracted or mentally "out of it"
- Having trouble falling or staying asleep
- Waking up tired after a restless night's sleep
- Setting unreasonably high standards for oneself
- Being perfectionistic or unduly self-critical
- Viewing minor setbacks as major catastrophes
- Having unexplained headaches, stomachaches, nausea, or diarrhea

• Sweating profusely or having cold, clammy hands
The complete diagnostic criteria for GAD can be found in
the Appendix.

GAD in Adolescents

Even very young children can be diagnosed with GAD. With
age, though, the quantity of anxiety symptoms tends to increase,
and the quality of symptoms tends to change as well. Compared
to younger children, teens with GAD tend to worry more about
events that occurred in the past as well as those that may happen
in the future. The worsening of these feelings often creeps up on
people gradually. By the time they're diagnosed, many say they
can't remember the last time they felt at ease.

GAD is one of the more common anxiety disorders. About
2% to 4% of adolescents meet the criteria for GAD, and it's
estimated that 5% of people will develop it at some point in
their lives. From early adolescence on, females with GAD out-
number males by about two to one. For most people, the disorder is a long-term condition that comes and goes. Often, it's
a stressful event that sets off a new round of worrying or causes
ongoing symptoms to get worse.

For Nia, her first bout of GAD seemed to be set in motion
partly by her sister's own struggles with OCD. "Nia became
symptomatic about year after her sister Claire did," their mother
recalls. "During that year, it was pretty stressful for the whole
family." But as Claire gradually gained better control over her
symptoms, and as the rest of the family got better at coping
with their reactions, the stress level in their home began to settle
back down. Meanwhile, Nia started treatment, too. Her problems with GAD didn't vanish, but they did improve greatly.

Looking back, Nia's mother is glad she sought help for her daughter when she did. Treatment for GAD may not "cure" the anxiety. In fact, the majority of people continue to have at least a few symptoms of anxiety even after being treated, and there is a good chance that the excessive worry will eventually return even after it is under control. However, treatment can still help teens with GAD feel much better in the short term. For the long term, therapy can give teens the skills they need to help them better manage their responses to stress in the future.

For the long term, therapy can give teens the skills they need to help them better manage their responses to stress in the future.

Other Related Problems

Among adolescents who do get treatment for GAD, almost all have at least one other mental or behavioral disorder. This is frequently another form of anxiety, such as a specific phobia, panic disorder, or social anxiety disorder. In addition, teens with GAD sometimes refuse to go to school or do schoolwork. Often, this is because of excessive concern about falling short of the high standards they've set for themselves.

A number of other conditions may coexist with GAD as well. Teens with GAD are at particularly high risk for depression. In part, this may be due to strong similarities between the two conditions. Both GAD and depression can lead to agitation, fatigue, trouble concentrating, irritability, and insomnia.

Research also suggests that teens with GAD have an increased risk of abusing alcohol or other drugs. Some studies have found that young people with GAD are more likely than their peers to start drinking alcohol at a young age. For many, this may be a misguided effort to assuage their anxious or depressed feelings.

Smoking and GAD

Research has documented a link between cigarette smoking and anxiety. One interesting study was published in *JAMA*, the journal of the American Medical Association, in 2000. That study found that heavy smoking in adolescence—defined as smoking at least 20 cigarettes a day—was associated with an increased risk of GAD, agoraphobia, and panic disorder in early adulthood. The reason for this association is still being studied. For some teens, though, the anxiety may come first. These teens may smoke to get the calming effects of nicotine as well as the social acceptance that comes from yielding to peer pressure. For other teens, the smoking may come first. It might contribute to the development of anxiety disorders by causing physical symptoms, such as shortness of breath, that can trigger anxiety or panic in predisposed people. Whichever precedes the other, once a teen is both anxious and hooked on cigarettes, it's likely that the two things interact to make each other worse.

Physical Disorders

The nagging worry and tension that go along with GAD may cause or worsen a number of physical ailments as well. Insomnia and fatigue are common symptoms of the disorder. Teens with GAD often have headaches, stomachaches, nausea, or diarrhea, too. There are a number of possible reasons for such complaints, however. If your teen is having any of these problems, he or she should see a doctor. It's important to rule out other medical conditions before assuming that anxiety is the cause.

Even if GAD is a contributing factor, that doesn't mean your teen's physical problems aren't real. The doctor may need to treat these problems at the same time that a mental health professional is treating the anxiety. For example, irritable bowel syndrome is a

Even if GAD is a contributing factor, that doesn't mean your teen's physical problems aren't real.

medical condition that often coexists with GAD. In this condition, the large intestine doesn't function properly, leading to abdominal cramps, bloating, constipation, or diarrhea. Stress aggravates irritable bowel syndrome, and taking steps to reduce stress and anxiety may help relieve the symptoms. But your teen's doctor may also prescribe antidiarrhea medications or changes in diet.

Causes and Contributors

Relatively little research has been done on the causes of GAD. However, it's known that the symptoms tend to get worse during times of stress. Some studies also suggest that the disorder

Sweet Dreams

Sleep gives the brain and body a much-needed chance to rest and refuel. For teens with GAD, though, bedtime all too often means lying awake worrying or tossing and turning through a fitful night's sleep. Sleeplessness and fatigue, in turn, just make anxiety worse. It's a vicious cycle, but you can help your teen break free by promoting good sleep habits. Encourage your teen to:

- Go to bed and get up at the same time every day, even on weekends and holidays.
- Spend the last half-hour before bedtime on quiet, soothing activities.
- Exercise regularly, but not within the last few hours before going to bed.
- Avoid taking naps during the day if that makes the insomnia worse.
- Get up and go to another room if he or she doesn't fall asleep within 30 minutes. Read something light or just sit quietly—no TV or computers. After 20 minutes or so, return to bed. Do this as often as necessary until sleep finally comes.

may run in families. And, as with other anxiety disorders, brain structure and chemistry seem to play important roles.

Stresses and Strains

GAD is an insidious condition that frequently starts out quietly and sneaks up on people slowly. As a result, it's hard to say exactly what set it off in the first place. However, it's possible that an accumulation of stressful life experiences may trigger anxiety in some people. For 12-year-old Becky, who was recently diagnosed with GAD, the anxiety seemed to build up gradually over a period of several years. Although it didn't reach a critical point until lately, one factor leading up to it may have been the death of Becky's father from Hodgkin's disease five years before.

"I do think the stress slowly added to it," says Becky's mother. "Becky won't talk about her father and how she feels. But tell her that she has to do the dishes when she doesn't want to, and she can have an emotional meltdown." Becky's mother is a young widow raising three children on her own, and a couple of years ago, she began having panic attacks as well. It seems likely that emotional loss and stress may have helped set off a chain reaction of anxiety within this family.

Once GAD is established, the connection to stress is often easier to see. Symptoms frequently grow worse during stressful periods. For teens, the trigger might be anything from moving to a new school or neighborhood, to coping with teasing or bullying at school, to prepping for the SAT. It's pointless to try to shield your teen from all stress, since it's an inevitable part of life. But warm, consistent parenting—coupled with therapy, if needed—can help teens develop greater resilience in the face of stress.

Genetic Factors

Research in adults indicates that genes play a role in causing GAD. One study published in 2001 found that the modest size of the genetic effect was about the same for women and men. As with other anxiety disorders, having certain genes doesn't necessarily mean that a person will develop the disorder. However, it may mean that the person is more vulnerable to becoming anxious if stressful life events come along.

One way in which genes may influence GAD is through inherited temperament. Youngsters with a "behaviorally inhibited" temperament are typically irritable as babies, fearful as toddlers, and shy and wary as school-aged children. These youngsters are more likely than their less inhibited peers to develop an anxiety disorder as they get older. Nevertheless, many shy, cautious children don't become overly anxious as teenagers, while some bolder children do. Childhood temperament is a risk factor, but it is far from a surefire predictor of things to come.

Physiological Factors

Like other anxiety disorders, GAD is associated with certain physiological features in the brain. Studies using high-tech equipment to produce images of the brain have shown that children with GAD tend to have an enlarged amygdala. The amygdala is the small structure inside the brain that controls fear responses and is thought to play a pivotal role in anxiety. Brain imaging studies in adults with GAD have also shown increased activity in the cerebral cortex (the thinking part of the brain) and decreased activity in the basal ganglia (a cluster of neurons that play a key role in movement and behavior). The precise significance of all these findings is still unclear. Taken together, however, they seem to support the theory that the brains of people with GAD are primed to overreact to stress.

People with GAD also seem to have low levels of two neurotransmitters: gamma-amino-butyric acid (GABA) and serotonin. GABA appears to help quell anxiety. Serotonin helps
regulate mood and sleep, and low levels of serotonin have been
implicated in both anxiety disorders and depression. The antianxiety and antidepressant medications often prescribed for
GAD work by increasing levels of these brain chemicals.

Diagnosis and Treatment

The more you know about the genetic and physiological roots
of GAD, the more apparent it becomes that it's a real illness,
not unlike diabetes or asthma. Just as for any other illness, your
job is to help your child with GAD get the best possible care
from the most qualified professionals you can find. It may not
be easy to accept that your child has a chronic disorder. However, the alternative is worse. In one parent's
words, "It was just really painful watching
my child be so anxious all the time to the
point of getting sick." While a diagnosis of
GAD is not exactly good news, it does open
the door to seeking treatment and relief for
your teen.

> "It was just really painful watching my child be so anxious all the time to the point of getting sick."

Getting a Diagnosis

The first step is to find out for sure what you're dealing with.
Since GAD often manifests itself in physical symptoms, you
may want to begin by making an appointment with your teen's
doctor. If you suspect that anxiety might be playing a role in
the symptoms, don't hesitate to bring up this possibility. Keep
in mind that diagnosing GAD can be tricky. The physiological

symptoms of GAD can masquerade as a whole host of other medical conditions. Also, the chronic, gradual nature of GAD makes it harder to recognize than a disorder that leads to a sudden, dramatic shift in behavior or personality.

Some pediatricians and family doctors are familiar with GAD, but others are not. If a thorough medical exam fails to turn up another cause for your teen's symptoms, the doctor may suggest consulting a mental health professional. Even if medical treatment is helping some of the problems, you may want to ask for a referral to a mental health professional if other signs of tension and worry aren't improving as well. Besides your doctor, possible sources for referrals include teachers, clergy, and support groups, such as the Anxiety Disorders Association of America.

To assess your teen's condition, a mental health professional will talk to your teen and observe his or her behavior. Since you are the world's leading authority on your child's past experiences and developmental history, you may also be asked to provide information that might shed light on the situation.

Of course, some degree of worry is a natural and even beneficial part of life. Worry really is nothing more than the expectation that something bad is going to happen, and that may be a completely reasonable expectation at times; for instance, if you have a big presentation due tomorrow and haven't started working on it yet. In this case, a little worry may be a good thing if it prompts you to get cracking on the presentation. The challenge for the mental health professional is sorting out short-term, healthy worry from the long-lasting, unhealthy kind that serves no useful purpose. To do that, the professional will look for evidence of significant distress or serious impairment in the teen's ability to function at home or school.

When it comes to finding help for your teen's GAD, sooner is better than later. Proper treatment may help your teen feel better, which might, in turn, help ward off complications, such as refusing to go to school or abusing alcohol or other drugs. The main treatment options are cognitive-behavioral therapy (CBT), medication, or a combination of the two.

Cognitive-Behavioral Therapy

Over the years, many kinds of psychotherapy have been used for GAD, but the one with the strongest research support is CBT. Studies in both younger children and adults have shown that CBT can be an effective treatment for GAD. Unfortunately, no controlled studies have yet investigated CBT specifically in adolescents with the disorder. But based on the results in both older and younger people, it seems likely that CBT is a good treatment choice for teens, too.

The cognitive component of CBT focuses on changing maladaptive or distorted thinking. Teens with GAD tend to see even minor setbacks as major catastrophes. For example, a single bad grade on a math test might make most students feel slightly disappointed or discouraged. However, for a student with GAD, it might lead to overly self-critical thoughts, such as "I'm hopeless at math" or "I'm stupid." These self-doubts might then snowball into exaggerated worries, such as "I'm going to fail the class" or "I'll never get into college."

Teens with GAD tend to see even minor setbacks as major catastrophes.

Distorted thoughts can lead to counterproductive behaviors. For example, teens who become overly worried about failing a class may start to believe that every assignment must be absolutely perfect and every test score must be 100%. As a result, they may fret so much over every detail of an assignment that they never manage to complete it. Or they may find excuses to stay home from school—not due to fear of what others will think of them, but out of concern that they won't meet their own overly perfectionistic standards.

The aim of CBT is to break this destructive chain of thoughts and behaviors. For starters, the person may record his or her thoughts and worries in a variety of situations. Later, the therapist and patient can discuss these thoughts, evaluate how realistic they are, and talk about ways to replace unreasonable thoughts with more reasonable ones. The student who got a single bad grade in math, for instance, might be helped to see that one grade in the context of other accomplishments. In the future, when thoughts such as "I'm stupid" or "I'll never get into college" come to mind, the student might try to replace them with more accurate thoughts, such as "I didn't do as well as I wanted this time, but it's just one test. I'm smart, and I've gotten good grades on other tests. One bad grade isn't a big deal."

The behavioral component of CBT comes into play when treating GAD, too. Since it's impossible to eliminate all anxiety from a person's life, the therapist may teach the patient specific skills to manage the physical symptoms that often accompany worry. For example, patients might be taught how to use deep breathing or soothing imagery to calm down when they start to feel tense and stressed out. Or, they might learn problem-solving skills that help them feel more confident about potentially worrisome situations. The basic concept behind CBT is that thoughts, behaviors, and feelings are all tied together. By changing one, you may change the others as well.

Exposure Therapy

Exposure therapy is a particular form of CBT in which people are systematically exposed to the situations that make them anxious. The idea is that the best way to overcome fears is by confronting them directly. It's easy to see how this might work for a teen who has a phobia of heights or a fear of public speaking. The specific fear cues for GAD often aren't as obvious, though, so the role played by exposure therapy may not be as prominent as for other anxiety disorders. Nevertheless, exposure therapy may be one part of CBT for GAD.

In exposure therapy, patients rank their fears and worries in a hierarchy based on how frightening the things are. Under a therapist's guidance, patients then gradually work their way from the least frightening items to the most frightening ones. In the case of a teen who is overly anxious about making mistakes on a homework assignment, an easy first step might be to practice deep breathing for relaxation before doing homework. The tasks would then get progressively harder. Ultimately, the teen might deliberately hand in a paper with a mistake on it. The goal wouldn't be to teach the teen to do sloppy work, of course, but rather to demonstrate that making an error isn't the end of the world.

Some worries may not be readily amenable to this approach; for example, if the teen worries excessively about terrorist attacks. However, let's say the teen avoids reading or watching the news because of concerns about terrorism. In that case, the teen might gradually work up to reading the front page of a newspaper or watching a news program on TV. At the same time, the teen could be encouraged to think more realistically about the likelihood of a terrorist attack in his or her community as well as about what he or she could do to cope more effectively with such worries.

Medication Therapy

A number of medications have proved to be effective for treating GAD in adults. Many work against depression as well, which makes them especially useful for people who suffer from both

Talk About It

Gloria's daughter Lexi has both GAD and OCD. She also has a number of other medical problems, including asthma, migraines, seizures, heartburn, and frequent constipation. The problems are many,
but Gloria says open communication helps keep both mother and
daughter from feeling overwhelmed. "From the start, I sat down and
said to her, 'This is what you have, this is the name for it, and other
people have it, too.' We also talked a lot about the coping strategies
that her therapist taught her. She's very clear that, if something makes
you anxious, you don't avoid it, because that will just make the
anxiety stronger."

Communication has also been the key to dealing with Lexi's older
sister, who in the past was often resentful of all the attention the
younger girl received. Says Gloria, "At first, her attitude was, 'Oh,
that's just Lexi being a drama queen.'" Gloria didn't dismiss her
older daughter's concerns, but she did try to explain the very real
mental and physical health challenges that Lexi faced. The message
apparently got through. Lexi's sister, now a freshman in college, has
grown more understanding lately, and she's even interested in studying neurology.

conditions. Several studies have suggested that the use of medication for the treatment of childhood GAD also may have positive results. However, these studies included other types of
childhood anxiety disorders in addition to GAD. At this time, there are several medication studies being performed to look at childhood GAD specifically.

Currently, doctors prescribe medications for young people with GAD based on the findings of both the pediatric and adult studies as well as clinical experience. The medications generally fall into four classes:

At this time, there are several medi-cation studies being performed to look at childhood GAD specifically.

selective serotonin reuptake inhibitors (SSRIs), serotonin–norepinephrine reuptake inhibitors (SNRIs), tricyclic antidepressants, and benzodiazepines.

- SSRIs—These medications are classified as antidepressants, but they're also widely used to treat anxiety disorders. They act by increasing the available supply of serotonin, a neurotransmitter that seems to play a central role in both anxiety disorders and depression. SSRIs include citalopram (Celexa), escitalopram (Lexapro), fluoxetine (Prozac), fluvoxamine (Luvox), paroxetine (Paxil), and sertraline (Zoloft). Well-controlled studies of fluvoxamine and sertraline have found that these drugs are effective treatments for GAD in young people up to age 17. On the downside, it can take a few weeks for the full effects of SSRIs to be felt, and they must be started at a low dose, since they sometimes actually worsen anxiety at first. Possible side effects include nausea, headache, nervousness, insomnia, jitteriness, and sexual problems. In 2004, the U.S. Food and Drug Administration (FDA) also issued a warning about a small but significant risk of increased suicidal thoughts and behaviors in children and adolescents who are taking antidepressants. For more information about this warning, see Chapter 7.
- SNRIs—Two newer antidepressants—duloxetine (Cymbalta) and venlafaxine (Effexor)—act on serotonin much like SSRIs do, but also affect another neurotransmitter called norepinephrine. These medications are sometimes prescribed for anxiety as well as depression. Venlafaxine, in particular, has been approved by the FDA for the treatment of GAD in adults. It can take a few weeks to get the full benefits of these drugs. The side effects are similar to

those for SSRIs, and the FDA warning about the risk of suicidal thoughts and behaviors applies here as well.

- Tricyclic antidepressants—These older antidepressants also affect the concentration and activity of serotonin and norepinephrine in the brain. However, they're more apt to cause troublesome side effects than their newer cousins, so they're usually not first-choice treatments. Tricyclic antidepressants include amitriptyline (Elavil), clomipramine (Anafranil), desipramine (Norpramin), doxepin (Sinequan), imipramine (Tofranil), maprotiline (Ludiomil), nortriptyline (Pamelor), protriptyline (Vivactil), and trimipramine (Surmontil). Possible side effects include dry mouth, constipation, bladder problems, sexual problems, blurred vision, dizziness, drowsiness, and increased heart rate. The FDA warning about the risk of suicidal thoughts and behaviors applies to these antidepressants, too.

- Benzodiazepines—These antianxiety medications are thought to raise levels of GABA, yet another neurotransmitter that seems to play a role in anxiety. Benzodiazepines include alprazolam (Xanax), chlordiazepoxide (Librium), clonazepam (Klonopin), clorazepate (Tranxene), diazepam (Valium), lorazepam (Ativan), and oxazepam (Serax). One advantage to these drugs is that they are fast-acting. Some people who take them feel better from the very first day. However, in the few small studies of benzodiazepines in young people, the results have been mixed. Some studies have found benefits, while others haven't, so for adolescents these medications usually aren't first-choice treatments used alone; however, in combination with an antidepressant, they can be very helpful for the acute disabling aspects of anxiety. Possible side effects include drowsiness, loss of coordination, fatigue, confusion, or mental slowing. If your teen is old enough to drive, he or she may be advised not to do so while taking one of these medications. If your teen has a substance abuse problem, be aware that combining these drugs with alcohol can lead to serious or even life-threatening complications. Also, benzodiazepines themselves can be abused, so their use needs to be closely supervised. For more information about the side effects of antianxiety drugs, see Chapter 7.

One additional option is buspirone (BuSpar), another medication approved for treating anxiety. Like antidepressants, buspirone acts by enhancing the activity of serotonin, and it has been shown to work against both anxiety and depression in adults. However, there is limited information about its effectiveness in young people.

The Best Treatment

CBT and medications each offer unique advantages. CBT doesn't carry the same risk of side effects as medications, and it teaches people skills that they can use for the rest of their lives. Numerous studies attest to the therapeutic power of CBT. On the other hand, medications attack the physiological roots of anxiety, and many studies have shown that they can also be quite effective. When weighing the pros and cons of these alternatives, it's important that both you and your teen clearly understand the expected benefits and risks of each. If you have any questions, don't hesitate to ask your doctor.

The best treatment for your teen is the one that's tailored to his or her individual

When weighing the pros and cons of these alternatives, it's important that both you and your teen clearly understand the expected benefits and risks of each.

needs. There is no one-size-fits-all therapy for GAD. Instead, mental health care providers look at factors such as the nature and severity of your teen's symptoms, the presence of depression or other complicating problems, and your teen's lifestyle and preferences when making treatment decisions.

If CBT and medications can each be effective on their own, wouldn't a combination of the two be the ideal treatment strategy? The answer is a definite maybe. For teens who don't get enough relief from either CBT or medications alone, a combination approach offers another alternative. Even for teens who respond well to one type of treatment, it's theoretically possible that the addition of a second type of treatment might boost the benefits. On the other hand, if medications blunt the fear response, it's also possible that they might reduce the effectiveness of exposure therapy, since this kind of therapy depends on confronting one's fears. This is another area in which research involving adolescents with GAD is sorely needed.

In the meantime, treatment providers make decisions based on your teen's needs, their clinical experience, and practical considerations, such as insurance coverage. One teen might receive medication at first to get anxiety symptoms under control, followed by several weeks of CBT, followed by occasional booster sessions of CBT as needed. Another teen might start with medication and CBT together, then continue taking the medication long after the CBT sessions have ended. A third teen who is highly motivated to work on his problems might do very well with CBT alone, while a fourth who lives 100 miles from the closest cognitive-behavioral therapist might rely solely on medication. Each of these is a viable option for some teens in some circumstances. Ultimately, the right treatment plan for *your* teen is the one that works.

Supporting Your Teen at Home

Since GAD is a long-term condition, it requires a long-term management strategy. Professional treatment is just one part of that process. The ongoing support that you provide for your teen is also a vital component. The more you know, the better you'll be able to help your teen navigate the ups and downs of GAD. As one parent put it: "My advice to 'new' parents? Read, read, read, read. Make it your mission to become as educated about the problem as you possibly can."

Worried About Worrying

You aren't responsible for your teen's GAD. As we've seen, a number of genetic, physiological, and environmental factors may conspire to give rise to anxiety in the first place. Once anxiety is established, though, the way you react is one of the many things that influence whether it waxes or wanes.

If you worry incessantly about your teen's worrying, you may wind up inadvertently fueling his or her anxiety. For one thing, you'll be acting as an anxious role model. Believe it or not, your teen still looks up to you and imitates your behavior. By letting your own worries rage out of control, you send precisely the wrong message. If you struggle with your own anxiety, one of the best things you can do for both yourself and your teen is to seek personal help.

Because you care so much about your child, you may also be tempted to become overly protective. It's natural to want to shield your child from things that cause distress. Many teens with GAD are especially good at bringing out the protector in people, because they're constantly

If you struggle with your own anxiety, one of the best things you can do for both yourself and your teen is to seek personal help.

seeking reassurance that everything is all right. Unfortunately, by "rescuing" your teen from challenging situations, you're really just depriving him or her of the chance to confront and overcome fears. Before long, you may have a vicious cycle going, in which your teen feels anxious, so you come to the rescue, which just makes your teen feel more anxious and less self-assured. To stop this cycle, you may need to temporarily check your parental instincts. Step back, and allow your teen to face some anxious situations on his or her own. If you have trouble striking the right balance between showing concern and fostering independence, your teen's therapist may be able to offer some helpful suggestions.

Time to Worry

One method of dealing with intrusive worries is to set aside a specific "worry time" each day. While this might seem counterintuitive, the idea is to set definite boundaries for the worries rather than letting them run rampant. Your teen might want to try this exercise. You can also use it yourself if you're finding it hard to focus on anything except your concerns about your teen's well-being.

1. Set aside two 15-minute blocks of time each day.

2. Spend the whole time worrying, letting yourself become as distressed as possible. Don't try to think of positive alternatives, and don't try to evaluate whether the thoughts are realistic. Just stew in your worries. If you run out of new things to fret over, return to the same old ones until the time is up.

You may find that it's hard to sustain this for a full 15 minutes. That's a good sign. When worries pop up at other times during the day, you'll remember how difficult it was to keep them up during the worry period. After a while, you'll be able to tell yourself, "That thought can wait until worry time."

Raising a Resilient Teen

Since stress is an unavoidable part of life, trying to shield your teen from it is futile. It makes more sense to help your teen develop the resilience to cope with stressful situations when they arise. Just as you encourage your teen to eat vegetables and be physically active, you can also teach your teen to make a regular habit of relaxation. Too many young people have schedules that would exhaust even the most workaholic executives. Make sure your teen has some time every day for simply unwinding and having fun in a low-stress, no-pressure environment.

Don't minimize the many sources of stress for teens. "Take their worries seriously," says one mother. Adolescents have to deal with rapidly changing bodies, emerging sexual feelings, and sometimes volatile emotions. Add to that new social pressures and increased academic demands, and stir in widespread societal problems, such as drugs and violence. You've got a recipe for considerable stress, which only serves to feed the anxiety and worry of vulnerable young people.

Talk to your teen about what's troubling him or her. If the level of concern seems overblown, help your teen see that his or her worries are exaggerated. Even if the situation truly is bleak, help your teen keep the problem in perspective. Let your teen know that brighter days lie ahead. An optimistic outlook is one of the most important weapons against anxiety and depression.

An optimistic outlook is one of the most important weapons against anxiety and depression.

While it's great to encourage your teen to look for silver linings, keep in mind that he or she may not be capable of seeing past the clouds until the anxiety lessens a bit. "Anxiety isn't something they can just get rid of by

Stress-Less Statements

"Don't worry, be happy" is a pointless exhortation. If your teen could simply do that, he or she undoubtedly would. Luckily, there are more helpful ways to respond when your teen expresses a concern. Following are some suggestions to get you started.

- "It's okay not to be perfect."
- "It's all right to make mistakes."
- "That thought doesn't seem like it's helping you right now."
- "You can handle being wrong."
- "That's not your responsibility."
- "You've done the best you can, and that's good enough."
- "Maybe it's time to take a break."
- "I feel like going for a walk. Want to join me?"

saying 'relax' or 'don't worry about it,'" says the parent of a teen with GAD. "And it's not something they can just wish away." That's where treatment with CBT or medication comes in. Once the anxious clouds start to lift, your teen may be ready for a more positive attitude.

Working with Your Teen's Teacher

When worry permeates your teen's life, some of it is bound to spill over into school. For one thing, it's hard for teens to concentrate on literature and science when they're preoccupied with thoughts of destruction and disaster. In addition, the physical complaints that often go along with GAD can interfere with school attendance, while perfectionism can stifle productivity and creativity. Plus, teens who are hampered by anxiety may find it harder to relate to their peers, and social ties are a very important part of the total school experience.

Yet it's all too easy for these problems to slip under the school's radar. Students with GAD are often so eager to please and motivated to excel that their suffering goes unnoticed until it becomes quite severe. As a parent, you may pick up on problems much sooner than a teacher who spends just an hour a day with your teen, and then only in a classroom filled with other students. If your child has a problem that you think the teacher should know about, don't hesitate to start a dialogue. You'll each be able to accomplish more if you work together as a team.

"Some parents don't want to do this because they're afraid it will put a stigma on their child," says Brenda, who is both the mother of a son with GAD as well a psychotherapist who counsels other parents. "But I always try to encourage them to keep the school involved and informed. In general, the more the school knows, the more they're going to be able to help your child. And you're going to really need that help if your child ever gets into a bind or has a crisis."

Toward Imperfectionism

Most parents would be thrilled if their teens not only did their schoolwork, but also checked it carefully. When teens have GAD, however, these positive qualities can be taken to a counterproductive extreme. Such teens may be so concerned about never making a mistake or getting less than an A that they find it nearly impossible to complete assignments or work up to their potential.

For such teens, a coordinated effort between home and school can help promote a healthy tolerance for human imperfection. Possible strategies include:

- Putting limits on revisions or erasures
- Setting time limits for turning in assignments
- Helping teens realistically assess the probability of a bad outcome
- Encouraging realistic thinking about the consequences of a minor mistake
- Tapering off the amount of reassurance you provide
- Being a positive role model by accepting your own imperfections and letting minor things go

Looking to the Future

Living with GAD can be trying for both the teens who have it and the parents who love them. "There were times when I just felt so frustrated, because I didn't know how to help," says one parent. By reading this book, you've taken a step toward reducing that frustration factor. You've read about some ways to support your teen at home and school, and you've learned when and how to seek professional treatment.

"There were times when I just felt so frustrated, because I didn't know how to help."

GAD tends to be a long-term condition that may get better for a while, then get worse again during times of stress. Treatment won't necessarily "cure" it permanently, but it can greatly reduce the suffering. For a teen who is consumed by pointless worrying or who is constantly tense for no reason, treatment can free up a lot of wasted mental and physical energy. The earlier your teen with GAD gets help, the sooner he or she can refocus that energy on the all-important business of learning, having fun, and becoming a young adult.

Chapter Five

Obsessive-Compulsive Disorder: Caught in a Mind Trap

It's common to hear people refer to themselves as "obsessed" with a hobby or "compulsive" about housecleaning. Everyone understands that it's just a figure of speech. Sure, you may find yourself preoccupied with the woodworking project in your garage or the unfinished novel on your desk when you should be concentrating on work. Or you may like the shirts in your closet arranged just so or your bed made a particular way. But these thoughts, habits, and quirks aren't doing you any serious harm, and you can usually set them aside if they get to be too much trouble.

For people with obsessive-compulsive disorder (OCD), however, simply turning off unwanted thoughts and behaviors isn't an option. They are plagued by repeated, distressing thoughts, called obsessions, that they feel unable to control. The thoughts aren't just excessive worries about real-life concerns. Instead, they're exaggerated fears and anxieties that have little basis in reality. Yet once these thoughts push their way into the person's mind, they refuse to leave no matter how much distress and inconvenience they cause.

Such intrusive thoughts give rise to so much anxiety that people are driven to find something—anything—that will bring relief. True compulsions are repetitive behaviors or mental acts that people feel compelled to perform in response to obsessions in order to prevent some feared consequences or harm from happening. For example, teens who are obsessed with contamination might wash their hands to get rid of the germs that they're sure are lurking there, despite the fact that their hands are already clean. Since their obsession is so intense, a quick splash under the faucet isn't enough to ease their fears. Instead, they may wash their hands again and again, or they may develop complicated hand-washing routines, such as scrubbing each finger a specific number of times. Afterward, their anxiety is reduced, but only temporarily. The anxious thoughts soon come back, and so does the need to wash their hands. It's little wonder that teens whose OCD symptoms take this form often wind up with hands that are red, chapped, and bleeding from constant scrubbing.

OCD can take myriad other forms, but, in one way or another, it always leads to negative consequences. One teen may become so preoccupied with checking and rechecking that her homework is in her backpack that she never actually makes it to class. Another may spend so much time silently counting everything in sight that he winds up isolated in a world of his own for hours on end.

One Family's Story

For 14-year-old Justin, the first hints of trouble appeared a few years ago while he was vacationing with his family in Canada. As his mother, Laura, remembers it, "We were walking along a path near the river when he reached out his leg and kicked me. I said, 'Hey, what did you do that for? You almost tripped me.' And he said, 'Well, I had touched you with my right leg, so I had to touch you with my left leg to even things out.'"

For most families, this would be one of those funny little incidents that is soon forgotten. In Justin's case, however, the compulsion to "even things out" soon became much more noticeable and disturbing. At school, he was disrupting class by flipping the light switch on and off repeatedly. "There was a three-toggle light switch in the classroom, and he had to get them all on or off at exactly the same moment," says Laura. At home, he had trouble typing on a keyboard or playing the piano, because he had to get the keystrokes exactly even, too.

Simply holding a conversation with Justin became excruciating. Laura remembers, "You would say, 'Hello, Justin.' And he would just stare at you blankly for a few seconds before he would finally respond." At first, Laura was mystified, but eventually she learned the reason for the awkward delays. "If someone said something, before the conversation could move on, he had to repeat it silently backward. So during those seconds when he seemed to be just staring, he was actually repeating whole sentences backward in his mind."

Justin began seeing a cognitive-behavioral therapist. He went twice a week at first, then once a week, then only occasionally for "refresher" sessions as needed. He also started taking medication to help control his symptoms. "He's doing very well," says Laura. Today, he plays saxophone, and he sometimes still gets the urge to even up the way he fingers the keys. When he's writing, he also sometimes wants to retrace the letters. The difference is that now he understands what's happening, and he and his mother have learned strategies for responding.

"He tells me right away when he's having problems," says Laura. In response, she and Justin usually work out a plan for helping him confront his anxiety. "Once in a while, I'll still bring him to the therapist's office for a refresher, but not often. Together, we can usually deal with it on our own now."

Rituals and Routines

As Justin found, it *is* quite possible to get better control of obsessive thoughts and the compulsive behaviors that often go along with them. It isn't easy, though. OCD is a tenacious illness, as anyone who has ever dealt with it will tell you. "It's an amazing sickness," says one father whose 16-year-old son only recently developed symptoms. "Things as simple as getting into the shower—things that you or I would take for granted—have become this elaborate ritual for him."

To understand the hold that obsessions can have on an adolescent, it helps to compare them to something more familiar: worries. When you worry, you feel distressed and anxious, but your specific thoughts vary from day to day as circumstances change. Obsessions, in contrast, are more stable. The same upsetting thoughts, impulses, or mental images come back time and again. Although the precise content of these thoughts varies from one person to the next, they often involve concerns about being dirty or sinful, or anxiety over something terrible that might happen. Each time the obsessive thoughts return, they stir up feelings of distress, fear, disgust, or shame.

Since these feelings are so unpleasant, people often try to neutralize them with another thought or action. That's where compulsions come into play. For example, consider a teen who is obsessed with the idea that her books will be stolen if she doesn't check her locker. She may try to neutralize this upsetting thought by checking to make sure that the books are still there. Eventually, she might wind up compulsively checking her locker many times a day—behavior that interferes with her ability to get to class on time and socialize with her friends between classes. At some point, she may recognize that her locker-checking has gotten out of hand. Yet she finds the compulsion to check it again almost impossible to resist.

Types of OCD

Obsessive thoughts lie at the heart of OCD. However, the compulsive rituals and routines they prompt are easier to see, so it is these behaviors that are used to classify subtypes of the disorder. Below are the seven most common OCD types. Keep in mind, though, that many people develop more than one kind of compulsive behavior.

. . . many people develop more than one kind of compulsive behavior

- Washers and cleaners—Some teens with OCD are obsessed with thoughts of contamination by germs, bodily secretions, or toxic chemicals. To counter such concerns, many wash their hands excessively—the most common compulsion in young people. Others develop complicated showering rituals or clean their room for hours on end. These same teens may also go to great lengths to avoid any contact with contaminated objects. For example, they might refuse to touch an object that has been dropped on the floor.
- Checkers—These teens are consumed with worries about potential calamities. To neutralize their worries, they repeatedly check to make sure that they've taken some protective action. For example, teens who worry obsessively

about burglars may check that the doors to the house are locked—not once or twice, but again and again. Teens with this type of OCD sometimes become stuck for hours in a repetitive thought loop of worrying and checking, worrying and checking.

- Repeaters—Like checkers, these teens are obsessed with potential catastrophes. The difference is that they feel driven to perform repetitive, protective rituals that have no logical connection to the feared event. For instance, a teen consumed by thoughts of his baby sister dying might feel as if the only way to keep this from happening is to repeatedly dress and undress until the disturbing thoughts pass.

- Orderers—These teens are plagued by a general sense of discomfort that arises whenever things are not in perfect order. To reduce their discomfort, the teens devote considerable time to ordering, arranging, straightening, or trying to make things symmetrical. Such teens may become extremely upset if their possessions are rearranged. To them, it's critical that everything be in the "right" place.

- Hoarders—These teens are obsessed with worries about not having what they'll need in the future. Some actively collect objects that most of us would consider useless. Others simply avoid throwing things away. Of course, many teens, like adults, are avid collectors. But while a typical teen might want to collect CDs, a hoarder might keep not only the CDs, but also the bags they came in.

- Mental ritualizers—These teens, like the others described above, engage in compulsive behaviors to keep the anxiety caused by obsessive thoughts at bay. The difference is that their rituals are performed entirely in their minds. The most common mental rituals are praying, counting, and silently repeating certain words or phrases. One mother says her son imagined a "flipping man," who flipped first one way and then the other, over and over.

- Pure obsessives—While the vast majority of teens with OCD engage in compulsive rituals, a few don't. Pure obsessives have repeated, distressing thoughts, but they haven't developed any compulsive behaviors for reducing the anxiety that results. Examples include disturbing impulses to hurt loved ones or shameful images of sexual acts that come to mind. These upsetting thoughts keep returning again and again, and the person feels unable to stop them.

Red Flags to Watch For

Do you think your teen may be suffering from OCD? These are some warning signs that your teen might need help:

- Having upsetting thoughts that keep coming back
- Being unusually worried about dirtiness or sinfulness
- Doing things over and over again
- Showing increased preoccupation with minor details
- Washing hands, showering, or cleaning excessively
- Checking door and window locks repeatedly
- Being inflexible about the way things are arranged
- Doing things a set number of times
- Hoarding or collecting an excessive amount of junk
- Taking much longer than usual to do simple tasks
- Acting as if daily life has become a struggle
- Seeking repeated reassurance about safety

The complete diagnostic criteria for OCD can be found in the Appendix.

Compelled to Act

While compulsions can be classified into broad categories, the specific forms they take are as unique as the individuals who have them. Following are a few examples that were shared by the parents interviewed for this book.

- "My oldest boy was putting on some deodorant, and the cap fell out of his hand and grazed Sammy's shoulder. It was like a medical emergency. The cap was infected! It touched his shoulder! Sammy had to take another shower and change all his clothes."—Father of a 16-year-old

- "We have a flagstone patio in the back, and the stones are a reddish color, a bluish color, and a grayish color. She could only step on the blue ones."—Mother of a 13-year-old

- "He does things in three sets of three, whether it's tapping the glass on the table, tapping the fork before he picks it up, lifting his eyebrows. It all happens in sets of three."—Mother of a 13-year-old

- "He can't throw anything out. He hoards stuff, even if it's broken. It's like, if you throw something out, it's going to change the whole order of things."—Mother of a 13-year-old

- "He counts everything. He counted the dots on the television one day until he got to the point where he couldn't look at the TV anymore."—Father of a 13-year-old

- "The first thing I noticed was when my son told me he saw some writing on someone else's test during spelling, so he purposely misspelled a word. He was worried about cheating when he wasn't really cheating. Then I kept him home from school for half a day, and he worried that he wasn't really sick. After that, he went downhill so quickly. He was tormented by his thoughts to the point where he couldn't stop crying, and he was banging his head because the thoughts wouldn't stop."—Mother of an 11-year-old

OCD in Adolescents

At one time, OCD was considered a rare condition in children and adolescents. Today, we know otherwise. Research suggests that as many as 1% of young people may have the disorder. Before puberty, boys are more likely than girls to have OCD. After puberty, though, girls catch up. The prevalence of OCD during adolescence is about equal between the sexes.

When younger children develop OCD, they often have trouble articulating the obsessive thoughts that underlie their compulsive behaviors. By comparison, teens are often more capable of discussing their obsessions. The most common obsessions in young people deal with contamination and dirtiness, and the most common compulsions involve washing and cleaning. Other common compulsions in this age group include checking, ordering, hoarding, and counting.

Unfortunately, OCD in young people often goes undiagnosed and untreated. For one thing, young people with OCD may be secretive about their symptoms. For another thing, although OCD has received more attention in recent years, many physicians, teachers, and others who work with young people are still unfamiliar with the disorder. This means it may be up to parents to bring the problem to the professionals' attention and, if appropriate, ask for a referral to a mental health care provider.

Tic Disorders and Tourette's Syndrome

Adolescents with OCD often have other disorders as well. Among the most common coexisting conditions are tic disorders and

Tourette's syndrome. A tic is a sudden, rapid, repetitive movement or vocalization that serves no useful purpose. Examples of motor tics include repeated, nonfunctional head jerking, facial grimacing, eye blinking, and tongue protruding. Examples of vocal tics include repeated, nonfunctional clicking, grunting, sniffing, and coughing. Vocal tics can also involve the repeated uttering of meaningless sounds or words.

Up to 30% of people with OCD report having had tics at some point in their lives. From 5% to 7% have full-blown Tourette's syndrome, a neurological disorder characterized by frequent, multiple tics. For Tourette's to be present, the person must have had multiple motor tics and at least one vocal tic at some point in the illness, although not necessarily all at the same time. On TV, people with Tourette's are often depicted as having coprolalia, a complex vocal tic that involves uttering obscenities. In reality, though, only a small fraction of people with Tourette's ever develop coprolalia.

Immediate family members of people with OCD have an increased risk of developing tic disorders. The reverse is also true: Close relatives of people with Tourette's and other tic disorders have a heightened risk of OCD. Research suggests that in some, but not all cases, OCD and Tourette's may represent alternate expressions of the same genetic variation.

Obsessive-Compulsive Spectrum Disorders

The existence of a genetic link between OCD and tic disorders, including Tourette's syndrome, seems clear. Some researchers have suggested that a similar link might exist between OCD and so-called "obsessive-compulsive spectrum disorders"—a group of disorders that, on the surface at least, resemble obsessions or compulsions and may respond to some of the same treatments as OCD. The concept of an obsessive-compulsive spectrum is still

One Boy, Two Challenges

Seventeen-year-old Ryan has both OCD and Tourette's. Over the years, his tics have taken many forms: humming, grunting, blinking, grimacing, shrugging, and jerking his leg, to name just a few. At one point, he even jerked his neck so much that he gave himself whiplash. Ryan's OCD has taken a variety of forms as well, including an obsession with contamination. "If he handled chemicals in science class, he was afraid that a residue would stay on his hands and get in his food and kill him," his mother says.

The combination of OCD and Tourette's made Ryan's early adolescent years quite difficult for both him and his family. Today, however, Ryan has learned to manage his symptoms and get on with his life with the help of therapy, medications, and his family's support. A high school senior, he's looking forward to college. His mother says, "Now, whenever we go to a TSA [Tourette Syndrome Association] or OCF [Obsessive-Compulsive Foundation] function, we meet parents who are where we were five years ago. For them, I think it helps being able to talk with us and meet Ryan, because they know we've been through it. It helps them, and it's gratifying for us."

open to debate, however. Although a number of mental and behavioral disorders are more common in people with OCD than in the general population, it's unclear which ones actually share a common genetic cause or biological pathway.

Conditions that seem to be associated with a higher-than-average lifetime risk of OCD include:

- Body dysmorphic disorder—A disorder in which people become so preoccupied with some imagined defect in their appearance that it causes serious distress or significant problems in their everyday life.
- Trichotillomania—A disorder in which people feel driven to pull out their own hair, leading to noticeable hair loss.

- Hypochondriasis—A disorder in which people become preoccupied with the idea that they have a serious illness, based on their misinterpretation of harmless bodily signs and sensations.
- Anorexia nervosa—An eating disorder in which people have an intense fear of becoming fat, so they severely restrict what they eat, often to the point of near starvation.
- Bulimia nervosa—An eating disorder in which people binge on large quantities of food, then purge by forced vomiting, laxative or diuretic abuse, or excessive exercise.

More research on the relationship between these disorders and OCD is needed. It's worth noting that there are significant differences as well as similarities among all of these conditions. Nevertheless, studies suggest that there might indeed be a shared genetic mechanism underlying OCD and some of these disorders. For example, a study published in *Biological Psychiatry* in 2000 found a hereditary link between OCD and both body dysmorphic disorder and abnormal "grooming" behaviors, such as trichotillomania.

Other Related Problems

It's not uncommon for teens with OCD to have another anxiety disorder, too, such as a specific phobia, panic disorder, social anxiety disorder, or generalized anxiety disorder. OCD can also occur alongside depression, although this may be less common in teens than in adults.

In addition, learning disorders appear to be relatively common among young people with OCD. Such disorders affect teens' performance in school or their ability to function in everyday situations that require reading, writing, or math skills. When students with OCD have learning disorders,

Table 2. What's the Difference?

OCD can look a lot like several other mental disorders. In addition, it's not always easy to tell the difference between OCD rituals and run-of-the-mill superstitions or quirky habits. This chart outlines some key distinguishing features.

OCD is sometimes confused with . . .	Compared to OCD, this condition leads to . . .
Generalized anxiety disorder	Excessive worries about real-life concerns. In contrast, OCD leads to exaggerated worries with no basis in reality.
Depression	Persistent brooding that seems appropriate to the person. In contrast, people with OCD regard their obsessions as inappropriate and intrusive.
Eating or body image disorders	A preoccupation with eating, body weight, or appearance. In contrast, OCD isn't limited to just these concerns.
Substance abuse or gambling addiction	An activity that people are driven to repeat because it gives them pleasure. In contrast, people with OCD are driven to repeat compulsions because the actions temporarily reduce the anxiety caused by obsessions.
Superstitions or quirky habits	Rituals or routines that aren't overly time-consuming and don't cause significant distress or impairment. In contrast, OCD is pervasive and leads to impairment in daily functioning.

they frequently have problems with handwriting, math, or expressive written language. Diagnosing a learning disorder can be complicated by the presence of OCD, however. That's because OCD itself sometimes interferes with the speed and efficiency with which students do their work. It can be hard to tell the difference between a student who is slowed down in school by OCD rituals and one who is hampered by a learning disability.

Causes and Contributors

OCD has been around for centuries. Writings from the Middle Ages describe religious compulsions and differentiate them from religious devotion. More recently, OCD has been documented in countries around the world. Not surprisingly for such a dramatic and pervasive illness, a number of theories have been advanced about the causes of OCD. At one time or another, the disorder has been attributed to everything from moral weakness to overly strict toilet training.

More recently, as scientific evidence has accumulated, the focus has shifted from emotional explanations to biochemical and genetic ones. Contrary to what you might think, there is no evidence that OCD is caused by childrearing practices or learned attitudes, such as an emphasis on cleanliness or a belief that certain thoughts are unacceptable. Instead, there is a substantial and growing body of research linking OCD to abnormal functioning of brain circuitry.

There is no evidence that OCD is caused by childrearing practices or learned attitudes . . .

The Serotonin Hypothesis

Brain imaging studies of people with OCD have revealed patterns of activity that differ from those seen in both healthy individuals and people with other mental illnesses. In particular, the brains of people with OCD often have abnormalities in circuits linking the orbital cortex, located at the front of the brain, to the basal ganglia, located deeper inside. Interestingly, other imaging studies have shown that these abnormalities in brain activity often disappear after treatment with either cognitive-behavioral therapy (CBT) or medication. Such studies provide graphic evidence that both therapy and medication can directly alter the way the brain works.

Serotonin, a chemical messenger that has been linked to both anxiety and depression, plays an important role in communication between these brain structures. One theory, known as the serotonin hypothesis, points to low serotonin levels as the root cause of OCD-related changes in brain function. The strongest evidence for this theory comes from studies that show a decrease in OCD symptoms among people who take selective serotonin reuptake inhibitors (SSRIs), medications that increase the available supply of serotonin in the brain.

Genetic Factors

Further evidence for the biological roots of OCD can be found in the family histories of many people with the disorder. There is a tendency for OCD to run in families. The risk of OCD is greater if a parent has it, and it's further increased if the parent developed OCD in childhood or if there are multiple relatives with OCD, Tourette's syndrome, or tics. You might think this tendency could be explained by children imitating the compulsive rituals they've seen their parents perform. However, in studies where both a parent and a child have OCD, the symptoms are usually dissimilar. For instance, a parent who compulsively cleans might have a child who compulsively checks or counts. This bolsters the argument that heredity rather than learning accounts for the family connection. So far, researchers have identified one genetic mutation that may play a role in certain cases of OCD. This mutation occurs in a serotonin trans-porter gene that helps regulate the amount of serotonin in the brain. A particular change in this gene reduces the amount of available serotonin and increases the risk of OCD or OCD-like symptoms. A few people have two different changes in this same gene, and the double whammy seems to be related to more severe OCD.

Of course, not everyone who develops OCD has a relative with the disorder. For those who do, however, the family con-nection is often a source of support and understanding. "In a way, I'm so glad that I went through the same kind of thing," says one father with OCD, whose 13-year-old son has the same condition. "When I was a kid, my parents didn't seem to know that they could do something to help. But because I've been through it myself, I un-derstand how important it is to get help for my son."

> "Because I've been through it myself, I understand how important it is to get help for my son."

Environmental Factors

As we've seen, OCD has its roots in biology and genetics. Parenting practices and family interactions don't cause the dis-order. Nevertheless, once the disorder is present, a teen's home life both affects and is affected by OCD. For one thing, young people with OCD often try to involve family members in their rituals. One father says that his 16-year-old son with OCD demanded that everyone in the household wash their hands in a certain way. "He would stand there and watch you, and if you did it wrong, he expected you to do it again and again and again until you got it right." This same boy also declared his bedroom off limits. After his brother went into the room one day, the boy demanded that the room be decontaminated.

"Change the sheets, change the pillowcases, sterilize the door-knobs, sterilize the TV clicker and the remote control for the stereo. Everything had to be sterilized," his father says.

No matter how irrational and inconvenient such demands might seem, parents are often tempted to comply in an effort to keep the peace and temporarily relieve their child's obvious distress. In other cases, parents go along because they are baffled by the bizarre-seeming requests and don't know what else to do. While these are understandable reactions, parents who co-operate with the OCD actually wind up strengthening their child's dysfunctional behaviors.

Strep Infection

Finally, some cases of childhood OCD may be set in motion by a strep infection. Observant doctors had noticed that, in a few children, OCD or tics started very suddenly and dramatically after a case of strep throat. This observation led to the identification of a disorder called PANDAS (short for pediatric autoimmune neuropsychiatric disorders associated with streptococcal infections). For a diagnosis of PANDAS to be made, a child must have either OCD or a tic disorder that started between age 3 and puberty. As time goes on, the symptoms must show a pattern of dramatic ups and downs. Typically, they worsen suddenly, then slowly and gradually get better over time. But if the child catches another strep infection, the OCD or tic symptoms abruptly worsen again.

Researchers are just starting to explore the mechanism behind PANDAS. In rheumatic fever, another disorder triggered by strep, the body's immune system goes awry. Instead of just attacking strep bacteria, antibodies produced by the immune system also mistakenly attack heart valves, joints, or certain

---

First-Person Singular

Want a glimpse inside your teen's mind? These memoirs written by individuals with OCD describe what it's really like to live with the disorder.

- Colas, Emily. *Just Checking: Scenes from the Life of an Obsessive-Compulsive.* New York: Washington Square Press, 1998.

- Summers, Marc, with Eric Hollander. *Everything in Its Place: My Trials and Triumphs with Obsessive Compulsive Disorder.* New York: Tarcher/Putnam, 2000.

- Traig, Jennifer. *Devil in the Details: Scenes from an Obsessive Girlhood.* New York: Little, Brown and Company, 2004.

- Wilensky, Amy S. *Passing for Normal.* New York: Broadway Books, 1999.

---

parts of the brain. It's believed that something similar might happen in PANDAS. Antibodies may set off an immune reaction that damages the basal ganglia, a cluster of nerve cells in the brain that play a key role in movement and behavior.

By definition, PANDAS is a childhood disorder. But as scientists learn more about the strep-OCD connection, it's quite possible they'll find that adolescents and adults can have immune-mediated OCD as well. Just because your child has had strep throat in the past doesn't necessarily mean that it's the cause of his or her OCD, however. Almost all school-age children catch strep throat at some point, but very, very few get OCD as a result. PANDAS is only considered as a diagnosis when there is a very close relationship between the start or worsening of OCD or tics and a preceding strep infection.

Diagnosis and Treatment

OCD is a brain disorder, so the best treatments for it are ones that actually change the way the brain works. Research has shown that both CBT and medications can have this effect. Recently, the lead author of this book was co-principal investigator on a study that evaluated the effectiveness of CBT, an SSRI medication, or a combination of the two for treating OCD in children and adolescents. The study was a randomized controlled trial— the gold standard in clinical research—that involved 112 young people seen at three university treatment centers.

All three treatments were more effective than a placebo (sugar pill) at reducing symptoms. Taken together, the results from the three centers showed that young people did better on a combination of CBT and an SSRI than on either treatment alone. However, for young people who were treated at the University of Pennsylvania, CBT alone worked as well as the combined treatment. This highlights the fact that the way therapists provide CBT is an important factor in determining how effective it is. The study also underscores just how successful state-of-the-art treatments can be. Among the University of Pennsylvania patients, almost two-thirds in both the CBT alone group and the combination group had few or no symptoms after 12 weeks of treatment.

Getting a Diagnosis

The first step toward finding treatment for your teen is to seek a professional diagnosis of the problem. While this sounds straightforward, it is complicated by the fact that a number of other mental and behavioral disorders can resemble OCD. To make an accurate diagnosis, a mental health professional will ask questions about your teen's past history and current symptoms.

The professional will conduct a diagnostic interview with the teen and observe his or her behavior. Since you know your child's current lifestyle and developmental history so well, you may also be asked to provide information.

Most teens have a few private rituals that make little sense, but are harmless and even comforting. For instance, they might turn down the bed the same way each night or knock on wood to prevent bad luck. Such rituals don't necessarily mean that a teen has OCD. To qualify as a disorder, the symptoms need to persist and cause significant distress or interfere with the teen's day-to-day life. Another cardinal feature that the professional looks for is "neutralizing." This means that rituals are performed specifically to counteract the anxiety provoked by certain thoughts or to reduce the chances that feared consequences will occur.

It's never good news to discover that your child has an illness. Yet once a diagnosis of OCD has been made, many parents say they are relieved to finally have a name to put to the problems their teen has been experiencing. "We had been alone, struggling, not understanding what was happening. So having a diagnosis was actually a big relief," says one mother. "Then the next stage was realizing that there was something to be done. It wasn't just this terrible thing that had happened. There was help for it, and that was the second great relief."

"We had been alone, struggling, not understanding what was happening. So having a diagnosis was actually a big relief."

Cognitive-Behavioral Therapy

CBT is the key element in the treatment of most teens with OCD. It helps people recognize and change self-defeating thought patterns as well as identify and change maladaptive behaviors. One particular form of CBT, known as exposure and response prevention (EX/RP; also called exposure and ritual prevention), has proved especially beneficial for treating OCD. The exposure component involves having people confront the thoughts or situations that provoke their obsessional distress, while the response prevention part means they voluntarily refrain from using compulsions to reduce their distress during these encounters. When people repeatedly face their fears without resorting to their compulsions, their anxiety gradually decreases over time. The anxiety lessens after repeated exposures to an anxiety-provoking situation, a process that psychologists refer to as habituation.

People can practice EX/RP either in real-life settings or in their imagination. Either way, they have a chance to put their fears to the reality test. When a ritual isn't performed and yet terrible consequences don't occur, it helps people recognize the flaws in their thinking. Once they've recognized that their fears are unrealistic, their thoughts, beliefs, and behaviors change.

For example, let's say a teen with a hand-washing compulsion was worried that touching "germy" doorknobs would make her sick. Even though she was forced to touched doorknobs every day, and even though she didn't become ill as a result, she might tell herself, "Yes, I touched the doorknob, and I didn't get sick, but that's only because I washed my hands so carefully." During EX/RP, the teen would not only touch a doorknob, but also refrain from washing her hands afterward. Over time, when she still didn't get sick, she would come to realize that her old belief about the necessity of constant washing wasn't accurate. She could then work to replace that belief with a more accurate one; for instance, "I've touched doorknobs many times before, and they didn't make me sick. Doorknobs are not dangerous."

Among adults, CBT is the best established treatment for OCD. For adolescents with the disorder, expert consensus guidelines published in the *Journal of Clinical Psychiatry* in 1997 recommended CBT, either alone or combined with medication, as the first-choice treatment. For many types of compulsions—including washing and cleaning, ordering, repeating, counting, and hoarding—the guidelines recommended EX/RP as especially useful.

A Typical Treatment Protocol

In a study funded by the National Institute of Mental Health, this book's lead author and her colleague John S. March used a treatment protocol for OCD that has since been widely emulated. This typical protocol consists of 14 visits spread out over 12 weeks. The treatment can be divided into five phases:

- Psychoeducation (weeks 1 and 2)—The therapist presents information about the nature of OCD, the risks and benefits of CBT, and the specifics of the treatment plan.
- Cognitive training (weeks 1 and 2)—The therapist teaches the patient to use cognitive tactics for resisting OCD. As one part of the training, patients are taught to use constructive self-talk to reward and encourage their own efforts to resist OCD.
- Mapping OCD (week 2)—The therapist explores the patient's experience of OCD, including specific obsessions, compulsions, triggers, and avoidance behaviors.
- EX/RP (weeks 3 through 12)—The patient uses EX/RP to confront anxiety-provoking situations while resisting the urge to resort to rituals or avoidance behaviors. The patient starts with situations in which the OCD symptoms are relatively easy to resist, then gradually works up to more and more challenging situations. In addition to

working directly with the therapist, the patient practices EX/RP in homework assignments.

- Relapse prevention (weeks 11 and 12)—The patient practices coping skills that can be used if the symptoms flare up again in the future. Such skills can help keep a brief flare-up from turning into a full-fledged, long-lasting return of symptoms.

Although this is a typical protocol, your own teen's treatment might differ a bit, depending on factors such as the severity of the symptoms, the presence of other disorders, the preferences of the therapist, your teen's response to the treatment, and the number of sessions covered by your insurance plan. Some variation is to be expected. But if your teen's therapy doesn't include the basic elements outlined above, he or she may not be receiving effective treatment.

As a parent, you'll have an active role in your teen's CBT. The therapist should provide you with information about CBT and explain how you can best support the treatment at home. You might also be invited to participate in some of the therapy sessions. If you've become caught up in your teen's rituals, the therapist should instruct you on how and when to stop participating. Stopping too abruptly might be counterproductive if your teen doesn't yet have the necessary coping skills to deal with the ensuing distress. In that case, the therapist will guide you in stopping your participation when your teen is ready.

As a parent, you'll have an active role in your teen's CBT.

Medication Therapy

Research suggests that some teens with OCD may benefit from receiving medication in addition to CBT. The combination of medication and CBT may be especially helpful for those with more severe symptoms and those with coexisting disorders such as Tourette's syndrome, another anxiety disorder, or depression. Fortunately, when it comes to studies of children and adolescents, more research has been done on medication therapy for OCD than for any other anxiety disorder. A growing body of evidence now supports the effectiveness of two types of medication: SSRIs and a tricyclic antidepressant called clomipramine (Anafranil).

- SSRIs—These medications are classified as antidepressants, but they're also widely used to treat anxiety disorders. They act by increasing the available supply of serotonin, a neurotransmitter that seems to play a central role in OCD. SSRIs include citalopram (Celexa), escitalopram (Lexapro), fluoxetine (Prozac), fluvoxamine (Luvox), paroxetine (Paxil), and sertraline (Zoloft). Large, well-controlled studies have shown that fluoxetine, fluvoxamine, and sertraline are effective for treating children and adolescents with OCD, and all three of these drugs have been specifically approved by the U.S. Food and Drug Administration (FDA) for that purpose. It can take a few weeks for the full effects of SSRIs to be felt, and they must be started at a low dose, since they sometimes actually worsen anxiety at first. Possible side effects include nausea, headache, nervousness, insomnia, jitteriness, and sexual problems. In 2004, the FDA also issued a warning about a small but significant risk of increased suicidal thoughts and behaviors in children and adolescents who are taking antidepressants. For more information about this warning, see Chapter 7.
- Clomipramine (Anafranil)—Clomipramine belongs to an older class of medications called tricyclic antidepressants.

Like SSRIs, tricyclic antidepressants also affect the concentration and activity of serotonin in the brain. Clomipramine, in particular, was the first drug to be systematically studied in children and adolescents with OCD. Studies found it to be effective, and it received FDA approval as a treatment for OCD in this age group. However, clomipramine is more likely to cause troublesome side effects than SSRIs, so it's usually not a first-choice treatment. Possible side effects include drowsiness, dry mouth, upset stomach, constipation, sexual problems, changes in appetite or weight, bladder problems, and increased heart rate. The FDA warning about the risk of suicidal thoughts and behaviors applies to clomipramine, too.

What to Expect

Different teens respond differently to treatment for OCD. In general, CBT is the cornerstone of treatment. But if CBT alone doesn't provide enough relief, the treatment provider may change to more intensive CBT or add an SSRI. If a combination of CBT and an SSRI isn't sufficient, the treatment provider may change to more intensive CBT, switch to a different medication, or add a second medication. "I think the important thing to know about OCD is that, with the right treatment, it does get better," says the mother of a 13-year-old with the disorder.

"I think the important thing to know about OCD is that, with the right treatment, it does get better."

Whatever treatment is chosen, the effects usually don't start to be felt for a few weeks. It's important for your teen to give any treatment a fair trial before deciding that it isn't working well enough. This generally means sticking with it for at least 10 weeks. For most patients, gains achieved with CBT tend to last over the long haul without the need for continuing treatment. On the other hand, for many patients, gains achieved with medication last only as long as the person keeps taking the medicine.

Supporting Your Teen at Home

One of the most helpful things you can do for your teen with OCD is to educate yourself about the illness. Your teen's therapist should supply some basic information about the disorder, but don't stop there. "I did a lot of research," says one parent. "I went to the OCF [Obsessive-Compulsive Foundation] online. And I got some books, and I did a lot of reading." A second parent says, "We have a good psychiatrist who put me in touch with the mother of another child with OCD shortly after my son's diagnosis. This woman was a world of help and, most importantly, she gave me hope that things would get better."

Keys to Communication

The more you know about OCD, the better able you'll be to talk to your teen about it. You can build your teen's self-esteem by making it clear that the problem is the illness, not the person who has it. Criticism just raises your teen's anxiety level and makes OCD that much harder to resist. On the other hand, when you approach any problems in a nonjudgmental way, you let your teen know that you understand what he or she is going through and that you're there to help.

Teens with OCD are often secretive about their symptoms out of a misplaced sense of shame, guilt, or embarrassment. As one mother says, "My daughter hid her symptoms. We weren't seeing everything that she was doing, and she wasn't telling us

Taking Care of You

It's easy to get so caught up in helping your teen that you forget to take care of yourself. Yet raising a teenager with OCD can be very stressful. Here's how other parents keep the stress from spiraling out of control.

- Enlist the help of supportive family and friends. "My daughter's OCD caused some tension in our family. My mother-in-law and mother didn't understand it. But my husband and I were on the same page, and that made a big difference."—Mother of a 16-year-old with OCD

- Join an in-person or online support group. "Joining the OCD and Parenting group was great. There were other people who would say, 'Yeah, my kid did that, and this is what worked for us and what didn't.'"—Mother of a 13-year-old with OCD (OCD and Parenting is an online support group available through Yahoo! Groups [health.groups.yahoo.com/group/ocdandparenting]. To find a face-to-face support group in your area, contact the Obsessive-Compulsive Foundation or Anxiety Disorders Association of America.)

- Keep a current crisis in perspective. "It's worse right before it gets better. There's this initial, awful period when the therapy isn't working yet, but it's like the storm before the calm. Once you get over that hump, things are so much better."—Mother of a 16-year-old with OCD

- Seek treatment for yourself if you need it. "I've seen therapists myself from time to time. Last year was so difficult, and I was crying every day, too. Things seemed so awful, and I was freaking out. Seeing a therapist really helped me."—Mother of a 13-year-old with OCD

about them. She was doing things that she couldn't stop, and she knew that was 'crazy,' so she didn't want us to know about it."

Encourage communication, but don't insist that your teen share more than he or she feels comfortable talking about. As time goes on, and as the treatment starts to take hold, your teen may open up more. When this happens, try to listen nonjudgmentally to whatever your teen has to say. Let your teen know that it's okay to talk about unpleasant thoughts and feelings as well as pleasant ones. Encourage your teen to examine these thoughts and feelings realistically. But refrain from offering simplistic advice, such as "Stop worrying!" or "Just stop it." Nobody dislikes the OCD symptoms more than your teen. If it were that easy to stop, your teen would undoubtedly have done so already. Instead, let your teen know that you realize how difficult it is, but that you're confident he or she can beat the disorder.

Nobody dislikes the OCD symptoms more than your teen.

Working with Your Teen's Teacher

So much of your teen's life centers around school. It should come as no surprise that OCD often affects social or academic functioning in the school setting. The degree of impairment varies widely from student to student, though. Some teens with OCD manage to keep their symptoms almost completely hidden at school. Others need only minor accommodations in the classroom, while still others require more extensive accommodations and special educational services.

OCD has the potential to affect academic performance in several ways. Students may be so preoccupied with obsessive thoughts that it's hard for them to think about anything else. Some students also develop school-related rituals, such as tracing and retracing their letters when writing, that interfere with their ability to get things done. In addition, some obsessions or compulsions are so time-consuming that they interfere with the ability to get to class, study, or do homework.

Should you talk to your teen's teachers about OCD? Discuss this with your teen first to gauge his or her comfort with sharing the information. There is always the risk that a few unenlightened people might react inappropriately. Most teachers are quite understanding and helpful, though, once they understand the nature of the problem. "My advice to other parents is to talk to the school a lot," says the father of a ninth-grader with OCD. "I've provided books to the school and given them information. I go to every school meeting. If I need to, I call the teachers or I make extra visits to the school. I think the schools appreciate it when parents are involved."

> "I go to every school meeting. If I need to, I call the teachers or I make extra visits to the school."

Small Changes, Big Results

Many students with OCD are able to adapt well to ordinary classroom demands, but others struggle at school. They may benefit from temporary accommodations and special services

---

A Voice of Experience

Ruth is both the mother of two teenagers with OCD and a therapist who specializes in treating anxiety disorders. She's also a firm believer in the importance of keeping school personnel in the loop. Ruth offers this example: "The other night, the mom of one of my own patients called me. She has a girl who's 12 who was just having an awful OCD night and couldn't stop checking and rechecking her homework. I said to the mom, 'Take the homework away. She's done. You can call the school tomorrow and tell them it was a horrible OCD night, so she couldn't do the homework.'" Of course, this strategy works best when teachers have been forewarned about the disorder. Even better, it's helpful if the parents and teachers have discussed in advance the kinds of problems that may arise and the solutions that might be needed.

that help them succeed at school until the OCD symptoms are under better control. The mother of a ninth-grader with OCD says he has benefited from having a 504 plan—one of two types of formal plans that cover educational services for students with mental and physical disabilities. (For more information on such plans, see Chapter 7.) "It allows him to take more time on tests and to type his homework. He also has a hall pass to just leave the classroom and go to the nurse or bathroom if he's feeling overstressed. And he gets at least 2 extra days to complete homework if he's having a difficult time."

Whether you have a formal plan or just an informal agreement with your teen's teacher, small accommodations can sometimes help your teen function better at school while you wait for a treatment to take effect or if the treatment is only partially successful. The needs of each student with OCD must be considered individually, and they change over time as the student's condition improves. These are examples of the types of short-term accommodations that some students with OCD have found helpful.

Students with contamination obsessions and washing compulsions:

- Letting students be first in line at the cafeteria.
- Seating students where they are first to receive handouts.
- Giving students an extra set of "uncontaminated" books to keep at home.
- Permitting students to go to their lockers early to avoid crowded hallways.
- Allowing students to go to the bathroom whenever they feel the need. Ironically, this may actually reduce the amount of time spent obsessing over not having access to a sink. When students are ready, limiting the number of bathroom passes may be appropriate.

Students with obsessions and compulsions that lead to perfectionism:

- Letting children make check marks instead of filling in circles on tests, for students with compulsions about filling in the circles perfectly.
- Permitting assignments to be typed or recorded on audiotape rather than handwritten, for students with compulsions about making their handwriting look just so. It may also help to let such students tape record lectures instead of taking notes by hand.

Students who are slowed down by their obsessions and compulsions:

- Allowing extra time for completing tests and homework, for students who feel compelled to check and recheck their work. Alternately, it may help to set a time limit for work, and accept whatever is completed in that time.
- Assigning shorter reading passages, for students with compulsions about reading and rereading sentences, or counting all the letters or words on a page. Alternately, students might be allowed to listen to books on tape or to have someone else read to them.

Remember that these are meant to be temporary measures, not permanent solutions. The goal is to help your teen function at school until treatment is successful.

Looking to the Future

OCD tends to be a long-term condition. In one study of children and teens with the disorder, 43% still had full-blown OCD two to seven years later, and only 11% were totally symptom-free. This study was done more than a decade ago, however, and the young people in it were initially treated with medication. The treatment for OCD is constantly being re-fined. Plus, evidence suggests that children and teens who start out being treated with CBT, either alone or combined with medication, learn lifelong skills that can help them maintain their improvement.

Even with CBT, your teen may not be completely cured of OCD. But there's an excellent chance that your teen can be helped to feel much better. Some residual symptoms might re-main, and these symptoms may wax and wane for years. How-ever, once your teen has mastered the basic techniques for resisting OCD, these skills can be applied whenever the disor-der flares up.

Discovering that your child has OCD can be very upsetting at first. As one mother put it, "You know that scene in *Titanic* where they're in the ocean hanging onto a piece of wood? I felt like my daughter and I were hanging onto this one piece of wood, and one of us was in danger of slipping off at any instant." This mother says the thing that helped boost her optimism the most was be-coming active in her local chapter of the Obsessive-Compulsive Foundation, where she had a chance to meet not only other par-ents, but also other people of all ages with OCD.

She says, "It helped so much for me to meet adults with OCD who had successfully overcome their symptoms and who now have jobs and families and kids. Because when your child is first struck with this disorder, you wonder if she's going to be forced to lead some marginal existence. And then you meet some of these people, and you realize that, with proper treat-ment, a large portion of people with OCD can lead very full lives and be very functional. And that was a real lifesaver for me, just realizing that her life was probably going to be okay."

Chapter Six

Post-Traumatic Stress Disorder: Failure to Recover From a Trauma

---

Imagine yourself as a young person who has lived through the extreme trauma of child sexual abuse, a school shooting, a serious car accident, or a devastating tornado. Now imagine yourself repeatedly reexperiencing that traumatic event in the form of flashbacks, nightmares, intrusive memories, or frightening mental images. For you, the sense of danger never really passes, so your mind and body remain constantly on high alert.

The persistent anxiety you feel after the trauma makes you want to avoid anything associated with that terrible event. You might go out of your way to avoid certain people, places, or activities, or you might simply try to avoid ever thinking or talking about what occurred. Perhaps you feel angry and distrustful of others, or maybe you feel shut off from your own emotions and unable to connect with family and friends.

You've just entered the mind of a teen with post-traumatic stress disorder (PTSD). The thing that makes PTSD diagnosis unique among the anxiety disorders is that it requires a precipitating event. This

> The thing that makes PTSD diagnosis unique among the anxiety disorders is that it requires a precipitating event.

Startling Stats

Adolescents are unfortunately at high risk for traumatic life experiences that can give rise to PTSD in some individuals:

- The National Child Traumatic Stress Network estimates that more than one-fourth of all American youth experience a serious traumatic event by age 16, and many suffer multiple traumas.
- In 2002, nearly 1.7 million young people between the ages of 12 and 19 were victims of a violent crime.
- In a large national survey, 9% of high school students reported having been raped at some point in their lives.

event is some form of terrifying ordeal in which grave physical harm to oneself or others either occurs or is threatened. Examples of such events include child physical or sexual abuse, rape, physical assault, kidnapping, natural disasters, terrorist attacks, serious accidents, life-threatening illnesses, or the sudden, unexpected death of a loved one.

These kinds of events are sadly common in the lives of American adolescents. Teens are twice as likely as other age groups to be victims of violent crime, and they are also at high risk for witnessing violence against others. Of course, not everyone who is exposed to a very traumatic event goes on to develop full-blown PTSD, even though many may have some lingering problems. But of young people who have ever experienced a trauma, it's estimated that from 3% to 15% of girls and from 1% to 6% of boys develop PTSD.

One Family's Story

At the time Jennifer was born, her parents were both addicted to drugs. They soon separated, and Jennifer remained with her mother, whose lifestyle with a new boyfriend grew increasingly erratic. Luckily for Jennifer, her paternal grandparents remained in the picture, and although they didn't yet know the extent of her problems, they were growing very alarmed by what they *could* see.

"My first thought was that she looked autistic," says Shirley of her granddaughter as a preschooler. "She was completely out of control, very hypersexual, and just a really strange little girl." But when Shirley took the girl to see a doctor, she was shocked when he suggested another explanation. Based on a physical exam, the doctor believed that Jennifer might be reacting to sexual abuse. Then on another occasion, Jennifer turned up with unexplained bruises from head to toe, leading her grandparents to strongly suspect that she was being physically abused as well.

Faced with abuse allegations, Jennifer's mother took the girl and dropped out of sight for a while. When the mother resurfaced, she was no longer willing to let Jennifer see her grandparents. Thus began several years of legal wrangling over visitation and custody. Eventually, Jennifer went to live with her grandparents. But it took another six years of court battles before her mother's parental rights were terminated and her grandparents were able to legally adopt her.

During those years, Jennifer was diagnosed with PTSD, which was traced to the sexual and physical abuse she had suffered as a child. Her symptoms may have been complicated by other emotional fallout from the abuse as well as the neurological impact of drugs her mother had used during pregnancy. Jennifer was plagued by recurring nightmares, and she always seemed to be on the lookout for danger. For a long time, it was difficult for her to connect with other people.

Once Jennifer reached middle school, she began getting into serious trouble at school. "She was always acting out—if it wasn't sexually, it was physically hurting people," her grandmother recalls. "I would get calls from the school while I was at work, and I could hear her screaming in the background."

The healing process was slow, but with therapy and medication as well as the steadfast support of her grandparents, Jennifer's problems gradually improved. One turning point came at age 14, when Jennifer's grandparents officially adopted her. "Once the courts finally severed her mother's parental rights, she got better quickly," Shirley says. "She was so enormously afraid of her mother. Without that hanging over her head, she was able to move on with her life."

Today, Jennifer is 21, married, and expecting her first child. Until recently, she also worked as a youth advocate for a mental health agency. "She's doing well," her grandmother says proudly. "She still has some emotional scars, but she's very self-willed. I've empowered her to the max." After a moment's reflection, she adds, "I feel like I'm very fortunate to have had the experience of raising Jennifer. She really changed our lives, and I learned so much. And man, that girl is brave."

> "She still has some emotional scars, but she's very self-willed. I've empowered her to the max."

Aftershocks of Trauma

Many upsetting and stressful things occur in the lives of young people. Parents divorce, grandparents die, classes are failed, best friends move away. While such events are certainly distressing, they generally don't lead to PTSD. To trigger the disorder, an event must involve at least one of these elements:

When Home Is Where the Hurt Is

Home should be the place where children feel loved and secure. For too many, though, it's the source of their trauma. Reliable data on the frequency of domestic violence and child physical abuse are lacking. However, it's estimated that from 3 to 10 million American children each year witness domestic violence against a parent. In addition, documented cases of child physical abuse total nearly 180,000 per year, but most experts consider this figure a gross underestimate, since it includes only cases that have been confirmed by child protective service agencies. All told, millions of young people are at high risk for PTSD because of violence they've witnessed or experienced in their own homes.

One mother of five, including a 19-year-old with PTSD, says she spent 11 years in an abusive relationship before getting out. During that time, she told herself that her children were okay so long as all the violence was aimed at her, not at them. Now she knows otherwise: "If you're in an abusive relationship, regardless of whether the abuse is directed toward you or your child, you need to realize that the damage is being done, and it's enormous. No matter how hard you try to shield your children from it, they know what's happening, and it *will* cause them problems in the future. Children see and understand a lot more than we as parents realize."

If you're struggling with violence in your home—whether you're the victim, a bystander, or the person having trouble controlling your angry feelings—help is out there. Good starting places are the Childhelp USA National Child Abuse Hotline (800-422-4533, www.childhelpusa.org) and the National Domestic Violence Hotline (800-799-7233, www.ndvh.org).

- Actual or threatened death or serious injury
- A threat to the person's physical integrity, such as child sexual abuse
- Witnessing the death, serious injury, or threat to physical integrity of another
- Learning about the sudden, unexpected death or serious injury of a loved one

At the time the event occurs, it gives rise to intense feelings of fear, helplessness, or horror. People who experience a trauma first-hand are generally more likely to develop PTSD than those who just witness or hear about it. Also, the more intense a trauma is, the greater the risk of the disorder. Long-lasting or repeated trauma—for example, ongoing violence in the home—is especially likely to lead to long-term difficulties. Symptoms are also more likely to be severe or long-lasting when the trauma is intentionally inflicted by another person.

> *People who experience a trauma firsthand are generally more likely to develop PTSD than those who just witness or hear about it.*

In practical terms, this means there is a much greater likelihood that people will develop PTSD after a rape, for instance, than after a natural disaster. In fact, research has shown that nearly half of women and two-thirds of men who have been raped go on to develop PTSD. The more danger people believed themselves to be in during the rape, the worse the symptoms are apt to be. When friends and family react negatively to what has happened—when they "blame the victim" or refuse to listen sympathetically to the victim's story—the risk is further increased.

In the Aftermath

PTSD includes three main types of symptoms: reexperiencing the traumatic event, avoidance and emotional numbing, and increased arousal or state of heightened alert. All three must be present for a diagnosis of the disorder to be made. Following are examples of specific symptoms that fall into each of these categories.

- Reexperiencing the traumatic event
  - Recurring memories of the event that are intrusive and distressing
  - Recurring nightmares about the event

- ○ Flashbacks in which the person, while awake, acts or feels as if the event is happening again
- ○ Intense emotional distress or physical reactions when exposed to triggers that remind the person of the event

- Avoidance and emotional numbing
  - ○ Efforts to avoid thinking, feeling, or talking about the event
  - ○ Efforts to avoid people, places, or activities that bring back memories of the event
  - ○ Inability to recall some important part of the event
  - ○ Reduced interest or participation in activities that were once enjoyed
  - ○ Feeling detached or estranged from others
  - ○ Restricted range of emotions (for example, the inability to feel love)
  - ○ Sense of a foreshortened future (for example, not expecting to live past 25)

- Increased arousal
  - ○ Difficulty falling or staying asleep
  - ○ Irritability or outbursts of anger
  - ○ Difficulty concentrating
  - ○ Constant vigilance
  - ○ Exaggerated startled response

Sooner and Later

Immediately after a terrible experience, some people have only mild symptoms that go away quickly without treatment. Other people, however, take longer to recover. Such post-trauma problems are given different names depending on how long they persist.

Post-trauma problems are given different names depending on how long they persist.

- Acute stress disorder—Symptoms that develop soon after a very traumatic event and last for less than a month. Although the symptoms are too brief to be considered PTSD, they are severe enough to impair day-to-day functioning.
- Acute PTSD—After a month, a diagnosis of PTSD can be considered. If the symptoms have lasted for only one to three months, the disorder is called acute PTSD.
- Chronic PTSD—If the symptoms have lasted for longer than three months, the disorder is called chronic PTSD.

In most cases, the symptoms of PTSD arise immediately after the traumatic event. Occasionally, though, they don't appear for months or even years afterward. When the onset of symptoms first occurs six months or more after the trauma, the disorder is called delayed PTSD. In such cases, the symptoms are often triggered by the anniversary of the event or the experience of a new trauma, especially if it reminds the person of the original event.

Red Flags to Watch For

Has your teen been through an extremely traumatic event? These are some warning signs that your teen might need help:

Acute Stress Disorder

Acute stress disorder is a short-term anxiety disorder that, by definition, lasts no more than a month. It starts with exposure to the same kind of traumatic event that can trigger PTSD, and it includes many of the same symptoms: reexperiencing the trauma, avoidance, and increased arousal. In addition, acute stress disorder includes dissociative symptoms, such as being "in a daze," feeling like a detached observer of one's own thoughts or behavior, and feeling as if the outside world is strange or unreal. To qualify as acute stress disorder, these symptoms must cause significant distress or impairment in everyday life.

- Having frequent, troubling memories of the event
- Acting as if the event is occurring all over again
- Going out of the way to avoid things associated with the event
- Developing physical or emotional symptoms when re-minded of it
- Being unable to recall important aspects of the trauma
- Worrying about dying at a young age
- Seeming emotionally detached from other people
- Startling more easily than before the event
- Having repeated nightmares or trouble sleeping

The complete diagnostic criteria for PTSD can be found in the Appendix.

PTSD in Adolescents

PTSD seems to be relatively common among adolescents. A recent national survey of 4,023 adolescents found that 3.7% of the boys and 6.3% of the girls reported meeting all the criteria for the disorder within the previous six months. Teens with PTSD are more likely than either younger children or adults to behave in an impulsive or aggressive manner. For the most part, though, their symptoms mirror those seen in adults.

Mark's two children—16-year-old Jason, who has mild mental retardation, and 13-year-old Brittany—developed PTSD after repeated sexual assaults by an older brother, who threatened to kill their parents if they ever told. Several months after Mark and his wife finally learned about the assaults, the older brother is in jail, and Jason and Brittany are

Teens with PTSD are more likely than either younger children or adults to behave in an impulsive or aggressive manner.

now receiving treatment with therapy and medication. Before the treatment started working, both teens showed the cardinal signs of PTSD: reexperiencing the trauma, avoidance, and increased arousal.

"Jason would have nightmares a couple of times a night, and they were both having frequent flashbacks," says Mark. These symptoms have subsided since treatment began, but the children and their therapist are still working on other symptoms. For example, several of the assaults took place in a basement family room while the parents were out of the house. As a result, both Jason and Brittany began avoiding the basement, and confronting this fear is one of their current goals in therapy. In addition, some of the assaults on Brittany occurred in her bedroom at night, after the parents were asleep. She is still very jumpy about being approached there. For now, her parents have gotten into the habit of talking as they walk down the hallway toward her bedroom so that she'll know they're coming. The healing process for the whole family is taking some time, but they're getting through it together.

Other Related Problems

All teens with PTSD have experienced at least one deeply disturbing event, and some, like Jason and Brittany, have been through multiple traumas over a period of months or years. It's no surprise that these teens often display a number of emotional and behavioral symptoms in addition to the classic signs of PTSD. Studies have found that young people with PTSD, like adults with the disorder, are at substantially increased risk for suicidal thoughts and behaviors, relationship difficulties, and other anxiety disorders, including social anxiety disorder, generalized anxiety disorder, panic disorder, and specific phobias. Physical symptoms—such as headaches, gastrointestinal complaints, immune system problems, dizziness, and chest pain—are also common. Several other disorders can coexist with PTSD as well.

- Depression—Researchers have found that as many as 41% of adolescents with PTSD develop depression by age 18. Often, the PTSD starts before or at the same time as the depression, suggesting that either the trauma or the PTSD symptoms were the root cause. In fact, many people respond to trauma by losing interest and pleasure in things they used to enjoy—one of the cardinal signs of both depression and PTSD. In addition, people sometimes develop irrational feelings of guilt after a trauma. They may feel as if the event was somehow their fault, even when this is clearly not the case. Such feelings are also typical of people with depression.
- Substance abuse—Teens with PTSD who turn to alcohol or other drugs may be trying to suppress disturbing memories, flashbacks, or mental images. Or they may be seeking relief from the constant state of mental and physical tension in which they live. Whatever the case, substance abuse is common in teens with PTSD. One study found that 46% of young people with the disorder became dependent on alcohol before age 18, and 25% became dependent on other drugs. Interestingly, being a trauma survivor alone doesn't seem to increase the risk of substance abuse. It's the distressing PTSD symptoms that appear to predispose teens to the problem. Unfortunately, any relief that these substances provide is temporary at best. In the long run, alcohol and drug abuse just worsen symptoms and make treatment more difficult.
- Disruptive behavior disorders—Attention-deficit hyperactivity disorder (ADHD), oppositional defiant disorder,

and conduct disorder are sometimes grouped together because all three can lead to highly disruptive behaviors. Such
disruptive behavior disorders are more common in young
people with PTSD than in those without the disorder.

ADHD—The key features of ADHD are inattention,
hyperactivity, or impulsive behavior that begins early in
life and may continue throughout the school years. Some
young people with ADHD are bothered mainly by dis-
tractibility and a short attention span, others by hyperactivity and impulsiveness, and still others by all these
problems combined. Certain symptoms of PTSD are similar to those of ADHD, which might lead to misdiagnosis
in some cases. But researchers have also suggested that
young people with true ADHD may be more likely to
develop PTSD after exposure to a trauma.

Oppositional defiant disorder—Most adolescents defy authority at times, especially when they're tired, stressed, or
upset. However, for those with oppositional defiant disorder, the defiant, uncooperative, and hostile behavior becomes a long-lasting way of life. Symptoms may include
angry outbursts, excessive arguing with adults, habitual
refusal to comply with adult requests, and deliberate attempts to annoy people. Once again, there is some symptom overlap with PTSD that could create confusion
between the two conditions. However, it's also possible
that PTSD might worsen any oppositional or defiant ten-
dencies that are already present.

Conduct disorder—Most teenagers test the rules now and
then. However, those with conduct disorder have extreme
difficulty following the rules or conforming to social norms.
They may threaten others, get into fights, set fires, vandal-
ize property, lie, steal, stay out all night, or run away from

Warning Signs of Suicide

Teens with PTSD are at increased risk for suicidal thoughts and behaviors. Be alert for these warning signs:

- Acting depressed, hopeless, or desperate
- Being preoccupied with death and dying
- Saying things such as "Nothing matters anymore," "I wish I were dead," or "I won't be a problem to you much longer"
- Giving away prized possessions, throwing out important belongings, or otherwise putting affairs in order
- Increasing use of alcohol or drugs
- Losing interest in his or her personal appearance
- Withdrawing from friends, family, and regular activities
- Experiencing a sudden change in eating or sleeping habits
- Describing himself or herself as a bad person
- Being unwilling to accept any praise or rewards

If your teen talks or acts in a way that leads you to believe that he or she might be feeling suicidal, get help immediately. Contact your teen's doctor or therapist right away, or call the National Hopeline Network (800-784-2433, www.hopeline.com) to find a crisis center in your area.

home. It has been suggested that young people who develop PTSD in response to violence may be especially likely to develop significant behavior problems. One possible explanation is that they've learned to identify with the perpetrator and mimic antisocial behavior.

Causes and Contributors

PTSD is triggered by a trauma, but it's influenced by the same kinds of genetic, biological, and environmental factors as other anxiety disorders. Such factors help explain why two people can live through the same traumatic experience, yet only one develops PTSD.

Past as Prologue

Research suggests that extreme stress early in life can affect how adverse events are experienced at a later date. In studies, rat pups who had been separated from their mothers for several minutes at a young age showed a much greater startle reaction to a stressful event months later than those who had never been separated. A human parallel may be found in people who have endured early traumas, such as child sexual or physical abuse, and who are prone to developing PTSD. According to one theory, extreme stress in early childhood, when the brain is still developing, may have lasting effects on a body system called the hypothalamic–pituitary–adrenal (HPA) axis.

Extreme stress in early childhood, when the brain is still developing, may have lasting effects on a body system called the hypothalamic–pituitary–adrenal (HPA) axis.

When a person perceives a threat, part of the brain called the hypothalamus is activated. The hypothalamus releases a hormone called corticotropin-releasing factor (CRF), which, in turn, triggers the release of pituitary and adrenal hormones. Together, these hormones set in motion a number of physiological changes that mobilize the body to respond quickly to the threat.

Research suggests that extreme stress early in life may affect the CRF-producing cells in the brain, leading to long-lasting overactivity of the HPA axis. As a result, a person might have a super-sensitive response to even the slightest whiff of danger, and this may lay the groundwork for both anxiety and depression.

Some studies have indeed found elevated levels of CRF in the cerebrospinal fluid—the fluid surrounding the brain and spinal cord—of people with PTSD. However, the situation is not as clear-cut as it sounds, since some children with anxiety disorders actually show HPA underactivity, rather than overactivity.

More Brain Changes

In brain imaging studies, researchers have found that the hippocampus—the part of the brain involved in emotion, learning, and memory—tends to be smaller than usual in adults with PTSD. It's thought that the hippocampus might shrink as a result of long-term overexposure to stress-related substances in the brain. Such shrinkage might play a role in the intrusive memories and flashbacks associated with PTSD. However, it has been found only in adults, not in children.

Another part of the brain that might be expected to contribute to PTSD is the amygdala, a small structure deep inside the brain that is activated by fear. Imaging studies of adults with PTSD have found that brain activity is increased in the amygdala and decreased in the prefrontal cortex, the part of the brain that inhibits amygdala activity. Selective serotonin reuptake inhibitors (SSRIs), medications that are sometimes used to treat PTSD, inhibit amygdala function, while cognitive-behavioral therapy (CBT) is thought to bolster the functioning of the prefrontal cortex.

Finally, as noted above, exposure to a threat sets off a whole cascade of physiological changes as the body prepares to react. Among these changes is the release of natural morphine-like substances in the brain that help blunt pain perception. Just as with CRF, researchers have found that production of these substances sometimes remains elevated even after the danger has passed. It's believed that this might contribute to the blunted emotions that characterize PTSD.

Genetic Factors

Some people may inherit a vulnerability to PTSD. However, this is a tricky matter to prove, since the disorder can't be assessed in relatives who haven't yet experienced a trauma. And even if the disorder is found in several members of the same family, it could be due to a shared trauma, such as living in the same violent household or going through a natural disaster together. As it turns out, studies suggest that environment alone can't account for all the variance in PTSD occurrence. But it's still important to tease out exactly what it is that's inherited. Is it a predisposition to PTSD itself, or is it instead a predisposition to some coexisting disorder, such as depression or substance abuse? Such coexisting disorders might lead to behaviors that increase the risk of trauma and thus contribute to PTSD, but only indirectly.

To date, the strongest evidence for a genetic link comes from studies of male twins who both served in the military during the Vietnam era. Genetics seemed to influence not only their PTSD symptoms, but also their chance of actually being involved in combat. Of course, individuals with certain inherited characteristics, such as physical strength and endurance, might be more likely to be assigned to a combat situation. However, it's also quite plausible that individuals with an inherited predisposition toward sensation seeking might be more likely to volunteer for hazardous duty. All told, one study of over 4,000 twin pairs found that genetic influences explained nearly half of the variance in combat exposure. Thus, it seems that genes may affect both behaviors that increase the risk of exposure to a trauma and the likelihood that PTSD will develop afterward.

Environmental Factors

PTSD is always a result of some traumatic event. A teen's home, neighborhood, and school environment have a big impact on the type of trauma to which he or she is potentially exposed. For example, a teen growing up in a neighborhood with lots of gang violence may face different risks than a teen from a safer neighborhood. After the trauma, environmental factors also influence the odds that PTSD will develop. Risk factors are characteristics that increase a person's likelihood of developing a disorder, while protective factors are characteristics that decrease the likelihood.

Table 3 contains some examples of risk and protective factors that have been reported for people who've experienced different

Table 3.   Risk and Protective Factors

The presence of risk factors doesn't mean that people will necessarily get PTSD, and the presence of protective factors doesn't guarantee that they won't. Instead, such factors merely raise or lower the risk. These are examples of risk and protective factors for particular types of traumatic events.

Trauma	Risk factors	Protective factors
School violence	Direct exposure as a victim or witness High rate of injury or loss of life Very disrupted or traumatized community	In-school counseling Referral to community mental health providers Family and community support
Life-threatening illness	Longer duration of treatment Advanced or recurrent disease	Good relationship with medical staff Accurate information about the illness
Natural disaster	Lack of family or social support Cold, fatigue, hunger Dislocation from or loss of one's home Lack of information about the event	Care and concern from recovery services personnel Information about what to expect and where to find help

types of trauma. Unfortunately, some traumas are so severe that even the presence of many protective factors may not prevent PTSD. Nevertheless, the more positive factors that teens have in their lives, the less severe their symptoms may be or the faster they may respond to treatment.

Diagnosis and Treatment

Many teens with PTSD gradually get better on their own over a period of months. But some continue to have symptoms for years if untreated. Any teen who continues to have significant symptoms for more than three months after the traumatic incident should see a mental health professional. If the symptoms are quite severe, treatment should start as early as three weeks after the traumatic event. The longer the symptoms go without treatment, the more likely it is that complications such as alcohol abuse will occur, so it pays to consult a professional sooner rather than later.

Psychological debriefing is a mental health service that is sometimes offered to survivors immediately after a traumatic event. Rather than treating PTSD, the intention of debriefing is to prevent it by helping survivors understand their feelings, reduce their distress, and prepare for what they may face in the future. Studies to date have provided little evidence that psychological debriefing actually prevents PTSD, but it may provide some immediate comfort and support as well as information about what to expect and where to find help. If your teen is offered psychological debriefing and chooses to take part, it could be worthwhile. However, such participation shouldn't be forced if your teen doesn't feel comfortable with it.

The actual treatment of PTSD usually starts only after a person has been safely removed from the traumatic situation. If a teen is still being exposed to extreme ongoing stress—for example, sexual abuse or violence in the home, physical abuse by a dating partner, or homelessness—addressing this crisis is the first concern. Once the situation has been stabilized, treatment for the lingering symptoms of PTSD can begin.

> Once the situation has been stabilized, treatment for the lingering symptoms of PTSD can begin.

Getting a Diagnosis

It's common for teens to be upset or have trouble functioning for a few days or weeks after a traumatic event. If symptoms persist, though, it's time to seek a professional diagnosis. A mental health professional will conduct a diagnostic interview with your teen to learn more about past experiences and current symptoms. At times, a symptom checklist may be used as a supplement to the interview. Since you know your child so well, you may be asked to provide information as well.

The accurate diagnosis of PTSD is not always a simple matter, however, even for trained professionals. The symptoms may be complicated by coexisting conditions, or they may be confused with other mental or physical disorders. And since doctors and teachers are not always well informed about PTSD, they may be slow to refer teens for psychological assessment and treatment. Fortunately, your teen has you in his or her corner. If you notice that your teen is struggling in the aftermath of a trauma, don't hesitate to ask for a referral to a mental health professional.

Cognitive-Behavioral Therapy

The best-studied form of therapy for PTSD in young people is cognitive-behavioral therapy (CBT). It focuses on both outward behaviors and the thoughts and beliefs that accompany these actions. The goal is to replace maladaptive behaviors, thoughts, and emotions with more adaptive ones. One crucial element of CBT that plays a key role in PTSD treatment is exposure therapy, in which a patient gradually confronts people, places, things, or memories that are associated with the trauma and are now safe, but still evoke intense fear.

One CBT program that is very effective with PTSD, called prolonged exposure, has been described by this book's lead author and her colleague Barbara O. Rothbaum. Over the course of 9 to 12 sessions, patients are helped to gradually confront a feared situation in real life. For example, a teen who was traumatized after being involved in a serious auto accident will be encouraged to gradually resume riding in a car again. Typically, patients start with easier steps (for example, sitting in a parked car) and gradually work up to harder and harder ones (for example, going for progressively longer rides). Over time, they come to realize that the feared situation is something they are able to face rather than avoid. Patients are also asked to confront traumatic memories in their imagination. For example, the therapist might have a patient retell traumatic memories until they no longer evoke fear.

Some people also develop unjustified feelings of guilt and self-blame after a traumatic experience. For example, the victim of a rape might blame herself for being in the wrong place at the wrong time, or the survivor of a school shooting might feel guilt for not saving his classmates. Through repeated recounting of the traumatic memory and discussion of it later with the therapist, the patient gains a more realistic perspective on the event.

> Some people also develop unjustified feelings of guilt and self-blame after a traumatic experience.

During CBT, patients may also learn specific skills that they can use to manage their symptoms of anxiety and stress. For example, in relaxation training, they might learn to control fear and stress by taking deep, even breaths; focusing on a soothing mental image; or progressively tensing and relaxing their muscles. Such techniques may give patients confidence that they can control their own thoughts and feelings rather than be controlled by them.

Although several other forms of therapy have been tried for PTSD, CBT is the best validated in scientific studies. One study published in 2004 included 229 young people ages 8 to 14 who had suffered sexual abuse. Almost all had experienced other traumatic events as well, such as being victims of physical abuse, witnessing domestic violence, or learning about the sudden, unexpected death of a loved one. All of the youngsters had at least several symptoms of PTSD, and a large majority met the full diagnostic criteria for the disorder. The youngsters were randomly assigned to received 12 weekly sessions of either CBT or another form of therapy. Those who received CBT showed greater improvements in PTSD, depression, behavior problems, and feelings of shame and self-blame.

Once your teen starts therapy, urge him or her to see it through. Facing up to frightening or disturbing memories in therapy is not pleasant, and it's understandable that many people want to give up. Let your teen know that you realize how difficult it is, but that this short-term distress is a small price to pay for long-term relief. Your encouragement can make a big difference.

Eye Movement Desensitization and Reprocessing

Another treatment, called eye movement desensitization and reprocessing (EMDR), combines elements of exposure therapy with directed shifts in attention. Patients are instructed to recall aspects of the traumatic experience while focusing on some back-and-forth stimulus. Originally, EMDR involved having the patient visually follow a therapist's side-to-side finger movements; hence, the name of the treatment. More recently, though, finger taps or sounds that alternate from one side of the patient's body to the other have been also included during treatment or used in place of the eye movements. Although the theory behind EMDR is still evolving, proponents claim that one key to its effectiveness is the side-to-side shift in attention. Several studies have failed to show that eye movements per se are an active part of the treatment, however.

There is some research evidence that EMDR can be helpful for PTSD. However, a head-to-head comparison of EMDR and traditional exposure therapy in adults found that the latter was more effective. Specifically, traditional exposure therapy was better at reducing symptoms of avoidance and reexperiencing the trauma, and it tended to bring faster relief as well.

Medication Therapy

CBT is the first-choice treatment for younger children and adults with PTSD. There is also some evidence that CBT is effective for teens who have the disorder. In contrast, there has been very little controlled research on the use of medications to treat young people with PTSD. Based on the limited evidence that's available, though, medications do seem to help some young people cope with severe or persistent symptoms. Medication is also helpful for treating other conditions, such as depression or different forms of anxiety that often go along with PTSD.

Expert consensus guidelines developed by this book's lead author and her colleagues recommend SSRIs as the first-choice medications for treating PTSD. SSRIs are antidepressant medications that are widely used to treat not only depression, but also anxiety disorders. A newer group of antidepressants, called serotonin–norepinephrine reuptake inhibitors (SNRIs), are highly recommended by the expert panel, too. If SSRIs and SNRIs fail to provide adequate relief, other types of medications— including tricyclic antidepressants, benzodiazepines, mood stabilizers, and atypical antipsychotics—are sometimes prescribed.

- SSRIs—These medications act by increasing the available supply of serotonin, a neurotransmitter that seems to play a central role in both anxiety disorders and depression. SSRIs include citalopram (Celexa), escitalopram (Lexapro), fluoxetine (Prozac), fluvoxamine (Luvox), paroxetine (Paxil), and sertraline (Zoloft). In well-controlled studies of adults with PTSD, fluoxetine, paroxetine, and sertraline have all been shown to be effective at reducing symptoms. In addition, one study of citalopram found that it worked as well for children and adolescents with PTSD as for adults. On the downside, it can take a few weeks for the full effects of SSRIs to be felt, and they must be started at a low dose, since they sometimes actually worsen anxiety at first. Possible side effects include nausea, headache, nervousness, insomnia, jitteriness, and sexual problems. In 2004, the U.S. Food and Drug Administration (FDA) also issued a warning about a small but significant risk of increased suicidal thoughts and behaviors in children and adolescents who are taking antidepressants. For more information about this warning, see Chapter 7.
- SNRIs—Two newer antidepressants—duloxetine (Cymbalta) and venlafaxine (Effexor)—act on serotonin much as SSRIs do, but also affect another neurotransmitter called

norepinephrine. Like SSRIs, these medications are sometimes prescribed for anxiety disorders, including PTSD,
as well as depression. It can take a few weeks to get the full
benefits of these drugs. The side effects are similar to those
for SSRIs, and the FDA warning about the risk of suicidal
thoughts and behaviors applies here as well.

- Tricyclic antidepressants—These older antidepressants also
affect the concentration and activity of serotonin and norepinephrine in the brain. However, they're more apt to cause
troublesome side effects than their newer cousins, so they're
usually not first-choice treatments. Tricyclic antidepressants
include amitriptyline (Elavil), clomipramine (Anafranil),
desipramine (Norpramin), doxepin (Sinequan), imipramine (Tofranil), maprotiline (Ludiomil), nortriptyline
(Pamelor), protriptyline (Vivactil), and trimipramine
(Surmontil). Possible side effects include dry mouth, constipation, bladder problems, sexual problems, blurred vision, dizziness, drowsiness, and increased heart rate. The
FDA warning about the risk of suicidal thoughts and behaviors applies to these antidepressants, too.

- Benzodiazepines—These antianxiety medications are
thought to raise levels of GABA, yet another neurotransmitter that seems to play a role in anxiety. Benzodiazepines
include alprazolam (Xanax), chlordiazepoxide (Librium),
clonazepam (Klonopin), clorazepate (Tranxene), diazepam
(Valium), lorazepam (Ativan), and oxazepam (Serax). The
available studies do not indicate that benzodiazepines are
beneficial for decreasing PTSD. Nevertheless, they are
sometimes still prescribed. One advantage to these drugs
is that they are fast-acting. Some people who take them
feel better from the very first day. However, these drugs
also have significant risks, so they are usually taken only

on a short-term or intermittent basis. Possible side effects include drowsiness, loss of coordination, fatigue, confusion, or mental slowing. If your teen is old enough to drive, he or she may be advised not to do so while taking one of these medications. If your teen has a substance abuse problem, be aware that combining these drugs with alcohol can lead to serious or even life-threatening complications. Also, benzodiazepines themselves can be abused, so their use needs to be closely supervised. For more information about the side effects of antianxiety drugs, see Chapter 7.

- Mood stabilizers and atypical antipsychotics—These medications help even out extreme mood swings. Mood stabilizers include carbamazepine (Tegretol), lamotrigine (Lamictal), and valproic acid (Depakote). Atypical antipsychotics include aripiprazole (Abilify), clozapine (Clozaril), olanzapine (Zyprexa), quetiapine (Seroquel), risperidone (Risperdal), and ziprasidone (Geodon). In small studies of children with PTSD, both risperidone and carbamazepine have been shown to reduce symptoms. While the specific side effects vary from drug to drug, they can be significant. Nevertheless, mood stabilizers and/or atypical antipsychotics may sometimes be helpful for people who don't respond to other medications or who have anger or irritability as prominent symptoms.

What to Expect

When teens have acute PTSD and no other coexisting problems, substantial improvement is often seen after just 12 to 20 sessions of CBT. In certain situations, as few as 3 to 6 CBT sessions may be enough. When medication is required, most experts recommend continuing it for 6 to 12 months.

While the majority of people with chronic PTSD benefit from short-term CBT, occasionally longer-term therapy is needed. This can take the form of either continuous weekly sessions or a few weeks of sessions interspersed with periods away from therapy. When medication is prescribed for chronic PTSD, it's usually taken for at least 12 to 24 months, and sometimes longer if the teen continues to have troublesome symptoms. Factors that increase the likelihood that longer-term treatment will be necessary include:

- Exposure to large-scale violence, such as war or a terrorist attack
- Long-term abuse or repeated exposure to extremely distressing events
- Trauma that is intentionally inflicted by another person
- Homicide or suicide of a family member
- Chaotic living situation or substance abuse by a parent
- Lack of trust and inability to connect emotionally with others
- Coexisting depression, substance abuse, or other mental health issues

Supporting Your Teen at Home

Seeking help for yourself as well as your teen will ultimately benefit both of you.

You play a critical role in helping your teen recover from a traumatic experience. The more effectively parents cope in the aftermath of a trauma, and the more support they give their children, the better their children are apt to do. If you're struggling with your own feelings, seeking help for yourself as well as your teen will ultimately benefit both of you. "Shelby's therapist worked with our entire family," says one parent. "It's easy to get overwhelmed from dealing with all of your child's issues. I think the therapist was the number one thing that helped us all get through it."

Perhaps the most helpful thing you can do is simply listen. This is harder than it sounds, since it can be wrenching to hear your child talk about going through a terrible ordeal. But your teen will benefit greatly from sharing the painful feelings and memories associated with the trauma. It helps your teen feel less alone to know that there is someone who understands what he or she has been through.

Don't force a discussion of the traumatic event, but let your teen know you're there when he or she needs to talk. You may find that your teen wants to rehash the same memories over and over again. Resist the urge to tell your teen to just forget about them and move on. While this might seem to be sensible advice, it may just make a bad situation worse. Your teen might end up feeling even more hopeless and alone.

Says one mother, "For the most part, I help my son by just listening when he needs to talk. I've learned not to push, but to let him open up when he feels like it." Says another, "A lot of these kids, they've seen a lot, and they've been through the mill. They don't want to be patronized. They want to be respected as real people with real feelings. You've just got to be there for them and listen to what they have to say."

Three Challenges for Parents

Sharon, who raised a granddaughter with chronic PTSD, went on to become a child advocate and parent coordinator for a mental health agency. Based on her own experiences and those of the moms and dads with whom she currently works, Sharon thinks the parents of teens with PTSD face three major challenges:

- Feeling powerless. "For the parents that I deal with, the biggest challenge they have is not feeling empowered themselves." To overcome this feeling, Sharon suggests educating yourself and talking to other parents who've been through the same thing. (To find a support group in your area, ask your teen's treatment provider or contact the Sidran Institute, a national nonprofit organization that provides referrals, education, and advocacy related to traumatic stress.)
- Accepting help. "It's crucial to know when you've had enough and you need other people to help you. If somebody else might know more than you about how to handle a particular situation, let them handle that piece." Sharon believes in building a support team of relatives, friends, teachers, treatment providers, child protective services workers—anyone with a stake in your teen's well-being.
- Letting go. "At the agency where I work, we have a parent whose kid is ready to transition into a different school setting, but the parents want her to stay where she is because *they're* fearful." Sharon knows how strong the urge to overprotect can be. "I had trouble with that, too," she says. "But the time comes when you need to let them move forward and grow on their own. They may surprise you."

"But the time comes when you need to let them move forward and grow on their own. They may surprise you."

Working with Your Teen's Teacher

PTSD can make it difficult to function in school. Compared to students without PTSD, those with the disorder tend to have lower grade point averages, more absences, and more conduct problems. Teachers and school counselors can often be invaluable allies when a teen is having trouble at school. But before discussing your child's PTSD with school personnel, talk to your teen and decide together how much information about the traumatic event you'll share. Respect your teen's privacy when it comes to sensitive issues, such as rape. You can always tell those who need to know about the PTSD without providing every detail of the trauma.

If you become aware that a specific classroom topic or situation is very disturbing for your teen, let the teacher know. Based on what the situation is and how far along your teen is in the treatment process, the two of you can then discuss how best to handle the situation in the future. In turn, ask the teacher to let you know if your teen starts showing signs of increased distress at school.

Disaster Relief

Teachers and school counselors play an important role in helping students cope with their feelings after a communitywide disaster, such as a severe storm or a violent attack at the school. If trauma or tragedy strikes your community, you might want to share these classroom suggestions from mental health experts.

- Encourage students to express their feelings through conversation, creative writing, and art projects.
- Provide information and answer questions about the event as best you can, but don't dwell on every awful detail.
- Respect the preferences of students who choose not to take part in classroom discussions about the traumatic event.
- Let students know about school and community resources they can access if they need further help or support.
- Reduce expectations temporarily, perhaps by giving less demanding assignments or rescheduling papers and tests.
- Help students feel safely in control of their environment by offering opportunities to make decisions in the classroom.

"Establish a partnership with the school," advises the parent of a girl with PTSD. "I do believe that it takes a village to raise a child. I knew what I wanted for her, but I was also willing to listen to what the teachers thought she needed. They really worked with me at her school." By teaming up with the teachers, you can help your student stay on track, academically and socially.

Looking to the Future

PTSD is relatively common in teens, but it also frequently goes undiagnosed and untreated. Many teachers, doctors, and other professionals who work with young people are not very familiar with the disorder. In addition, many teens don't seek assistance, because they don't realize they have a problem or that something can be done to help them feel better. It's also natural to want to avoid the upsetting thoughts and feelings associated with a trauma. Without treatment, PTSD often goes away on its own shortly after the trauma. But in some cases, it lingers for years, causing substantial suffering.

By helping your teen with PTSD get the treatment he or she needs, you greatly improve the odds of a good outcome. Even with treatment, some symptoms may not disappear completely. Other symptoms may come and go over months or years. But much more is known today about the effective treatment of PTSD than was known just a decade ago. The chances are excellent that your teen's symptoms can be substantially reduced with CBT and perhaps medication.

"There are going to be good days, and there are going to be bad days," says one mother. "You've just got to be there for them and listen to them." And trust that things will get better in time. For both you and your teen, brighter days lie ahead.

Chapter Seven

Treatment and Recovery:
A Close-Up of the Process

Some parents say they experienced shock and denial when their teen was first diagnosed with an anxiety disorder. "It was really out of the blue for us," says the mother of a 16-year-old with obsessive-compulsive disorder (OCD). "We knew something was wrong, but this was not what we had been expecting. None of us accepted it immediately—not me or my daughter or my husband. Speaking for myself, I had all these stereotypes in my head about the illness. I didn't know enough about it, so I overreacted."

Others say they felt relief at finally having a name to put to their teen's puzzling behavior. And still others say they felt vindicated to have a professional confirm what they had suspected for some time. Whatever your own first thought might have been, it was probably soon followed by a string of questions: Where can I find a first-rate therapist for my teen? What are the pros and cons of medication? How will I pay for my teen's care? And what can I do to help my teen succeed in school?

None of these questions has a simple answer. But the more informed you are about your options, the better decisions you'll be able to make about such complicated issues. In this chapter, you'll find essential facts for making sound treatment and educational decisions, no matter which anxiety disorder your teen might have.

Getting a Diagnosis

The first step toward finding help for your teen is getting an accurate diagnosis of the problem. To assess the situation, a mental health professional will conduct a diagnostic interview with your teen. Often, this takes the form of a structured interview, in which the questions that are asked and the order in which they're presented are predetermined. The goal is to allow the professional to pinpoint the nature, severity, and duration of your teen's symptoms. This information can then be used to compare the symptoms that your teen is experiencing to the diagnostic criteria in the *DSM-IV-TR* (short for *Diagnostic and Statistical Manual of Mental Disorders*, Fourth Edition, Text Revision), a manual published by the American Psychiatric Association. Mental health professionals from many fields use this manual for diagnosing all kinds of mental disorders. A simplified version of the *DSM-IV-TR* criteria for the various anxiety disorders can be found in the Appendix. In addition to the verbal interview, your teen might be asked to fill out a paper-and-pencil questionnaire that further explores problems, symptoms, and daily behavior.

You'll be asked to provide information as well, so come prepared. Among other things, you may be asked about your teen's:

- Current problems and symptoms
- Medical history and general physical health
- Previous mental health diagnoses and treatments, if any

- Family history of mental health problems
- Physical and mental development
- Relationships with family and friends

During the assessment process, the professional will closely observe your teen's behavior. Of course, the professional only sees your teen for a brief time in a single setting, so he or she doesn't get the full picture the way a parent does. For this reason, you may be asked to fill out a behavior rating scale, on which you report the behaviors you've observed and how frequently they've occurred.

At times, it may be helpful to get the perspective of other significant adults in your teen's life as well. With your permission, such adults—for example, teachers, the school counselor, or your teen's doctor—may be contacted and asked to also fill out a behavior rating scale or provide other information.

The professional only sees your teen for a brief time in a single setting, so he or she doesn't get the full picture the way a parent does.

Finding Appropriate Therapy

Once a diagnosis has been made, the next challenge is finding appropriate treatment for your teen. Cognitive-behavioral therapy (CBT), including exposure therapy, is the best-established treatment for anxiety disorders in adolescents. In scientific studies, its effectiveness has been shown time and again. One advantage of CBT is that it doesn't carry the same risk of side effects as medications. It also teaches people anxiety-management skills that they can continue to use for the rest of their lives. For those who don't get enough relief from CBT alone or do not

Participating in Research

It's possible that your teen may have the opportunity to participate in a research project evaluating treatments for anxiety. As the parent of a minor, you'll be fully informed about the potential benefits and risks of participation, and you'll be required to give your consent before your teen can volunteer. One advantage to taking part in a study is that it may give your teen access to free, high-quality care. On the downside, there may be some inconvenience to you. For example, you might need to travel some distance to a treatment center or be available for follow-up appointments.

respond to this form of treatment, a medication may improve the treatment outcome by being added to CBT. In some cases, medication used alone may be effective.

One potential drawback to CBT is that optimal results depend on access to a cognitive-behavioral therapist, preferably one with experience treating adolescents. In many parts of the country, such therapists are few and far between. One mother who volunteers to answer phones for an OCD support group says, "I talk to parents all the time whose teenagers have just become symptomatic, and the biggest, biggest problem they have is finding a qualified treatment provider."

CBT also requires the active participation of the patient. If your teen is very resistant to the idea of therapy or unwilling to do homework assigned by the therapist, he or she may not get the best results. Exposure therapy, in particular, requires confronting one's fears, which can lead to a short-term increase in anxiety and distress that some teens may not be willing to tolerate. However, many teens with anxiety disorders are eager to find relief from their symptoms, and others come around once they discover that CBT really does help.

As a parent, you can encourage your teen's efforts to gradually confront his or her fears, even if that sometimes means checking your protective impulses. You can also let your teen know how proud you are when he or she successfully achieves a goal. In addition, you can serve as a positive role model, by building your own self-confidence, facing your own unrealistic fears, and seeking help for problems when you need it.

Choosing a Therapist

CBT is provided by mental health professionals from a variety of fields, including psychologists, psychiatrists, and clinical social workers. When choosing someone to provide treatment for your teen, factors to consider include the therapist's experience with exposure therapy, his or her expertise in working with young people, and your and your teen's comfort level with the therapist.

Relaxation techniques, such as imagery and breathing exercises, are sometimes taught as one component of CBT. They offer teens useful skills for managing the physiological effects of fear and stress. However, there is no evidence that relaxation training alone is sufficient to treat anxiety disorders. Instead, research points to exposure therapy as the critical component of CBT where anxiety disorders are involved. Make sure this is the therapist's focus as well.

"I didn't know where to start looking for the right kind of therapist," says one mother, who had heard about exposure therapy for OCD (often called exposure and response prevention). "I started just calling therapists at random, and I would ask them, 'Do you do this kind of therapy?' I called about 20 of them before I finally contacted a woman who put me in touch

"I finally contacted a woman who put me in touch with the local chapter of the Obsessive-Compulsive Foundation. I called them, and they referred me to a therapist right away."

with the local chapter of the Obsessive-Compulsive Foundation. I called them, and they referred me to a therapist right away." Other good sources for referrals include the Anxiety Disorders Association of America and the Association for Advancement of Behavior Therapy, both of which provide searchable lists of treatment providers on their websites. You might also contact your local community mental heath clinic and ask if they can recommend any therapists who specialize in treating anxiety disorders. Once you've gathered a list of therapist names, these are some questions to ask:

- What kind of licensure and credentials do you have?
- Do you consider yourself a specialist in anxiety disorders?
- How many of your patients have my teen's particular disorder?
- How many of your patients are adolescents or children?
- How much experience do you have with CBT, including exposure therapy?
- Will you or a staff member make home visits to do exposures if needed?
- Can you prescribe medication? If not, are you willing to coordinate care with a prescriber if my teen is already on medication or if medication later turns out to be necessary?
- How frequent will treatment sessions be, and how long will they last?
- How many sessions do you expect will be required?
- Do you involve family members in the therapy?
- What are your fees? Do you have a sliding scale for people with limited financial resources? Are you involved in any

research studies under which my teen might be eligible to receive treatment for free?

- What kinds of insurance plans do you accept?
- Where is your office located, and what are your hours?

Of all these considerations, finding someone with substantial experience in treating anxiety disorders is paramount. "Find

Table 4.   Therapists at a Glance

Mental health professionals from several fields provide therapy. However, not all are familiar with research-based treatments for anxiety disorders, so be sure to ask about the treatment approach when choosing a therapist for your teen.

Providers of therapy	May prescribe medication?	Credentials to look for
Psychologists	In New Mexico and Louisiana only, with advanced training	State license
Psychiatrists	Yes	State license and board-certified (or board-eligible) by the American Board of Psychiatry and Neurology
Psychiatric nurses	Yes, with advanced training	State license and certification by the American Nurses Credentialing Center
Clinical social workers	No	State license; may be a member of the Academy of Certified Social Workers
Mental health counselors	No	State license or certified by the National Academy of Certified Clinical Mental Health Counselors
Marriage and family therapists	No	State license

a therapist who eats, sleeps, and breathes this," advises one parent. "Right now, we have about an hour and a half's drive to see the therapist," says another. "But when it's your child, you'll do whatever it takes."

Pros and Cons of Medication

If CBT alone fails to provide sufficient relief, medication is often prescribed along with it. Medication may also be useful if your teen is unwilling to participate in therapy or doesn't have access to a qualified therapist. Also there are times when CBT does not work for a particular adolescent. In addition, medication may be helpful if your teen has a coexisting disorder, such as depression or attention-deficit hyperactivity disorder, that tends to respond well to drug treatment.

When symptoms are moderate to severe, medication can often suppress them enough to make it easier to concentrate on therapy. One mother says that her daughter initially started treatment with CBT alone, but grew frustrated after several weeks of uneven results. For every step forward, there seemed to be one or two backward. "When we added medication, that was really a turning point," says this mother. "The medication strengthened her so that she could make the behavioral therapy work for her in a consistent way."

More research is needed on the safety and effectiveness of specific medications for treating anxiety disorders in adolescents. Nevertheless, the research that's currently available, coupled with clinical experience, indicates that medication can be helpful and safe in many cases. One drawback is the risk of unwanted side effects. In addition, different people respond differently to the same drug, based on individual factors such as age, sex, weight, body chemistry, and general health. Finding the right medication and dosage may require some trial and error.

Selective serotonin reuptake inhibitors (SSRIs) are often the medications of choice for treating anxiety disorders in adolescents. These medications are effective against both anxiety and depression, and most of the side effects tend to be mild. However, the U.S. Food and Drug Administration (FDA) recently issued a warning about a small but significant risk of increased suicidal thoughts and behaviors in young people who are taking SSRIs and other antidepressants. This underscores the importance of carefully weighing the potential benefits and risks of any medication when considering your teen's treatment options.

Antidepressant Warning

In 2004, the FDA directed makers of all antidepressants to add stronger warning statements to their product labeling about a small but significant risk of increased suicidal thoughts and behaviors in children and adolescents who take these medications. As a result, physicians who choose to prescribe antidepressants for young people are strongly encouraged to monitor their patients closely. You can help with this, too. If your teen is taking an antidepressant, call the doctor right away if you notice any of these warning signs:

- suicidal talk or behavior
- increased anxiety or depression
- extreme restlessness or agitation
- increased panic attacks
- trouble sleeping
- increased irritability, aggression, or violence
- impulsive risk-taking
- extreme hyperactivity or talkativeness
- unusual changes in behavior.

While adverse effects are a significant concern, this risk must be balanced against the risk of not treating your teen's disorder adequately. When symptoms go untreated, they can cause substantial distress and interfere with day-to-day life. In addition, they can interfere with emotional and social growth during this critical period in your teen's development.

Getting the Facts

Prescriptions for antidepressants and other anxiety medications can be written by primary care physicians, such as pediatricians and family physicians, as well as a few other health care providers (see chart on page 165). However, psychiatrists—medical doctors who specialize in the diagnosis and treatment of mental disorders—are the specialists with the most knowledge and training in the use of such medications.

"My son's pediatrician doesn't feel comfortable writing a prescription for Zoloft [an SSRI]," says one mother. "That's not his cup of tea. So we see the psychiatrist whenever we need to, but no less than once or twice a year. I also have to write the psychiatrist once a month to update him on how my son's doing. And I can always call him if there's something wrong." One thing she especially appreciates about this psychiatrist is his willingness to answer all her questions. Plus, she says, "he really listens to what I have to say."

If medication is prescribed, tell the doctor about any other prescription medications, over-the-counter medicines, or herbal supplements your teen is taking, since some medications interact harmfully with each other. Also let the doctor know about any drug allergies your teen has. Then make sure you have all the facts you need. These are some important questions to ask:

- What are the generic and brand names of the medication?
- What is it supposed to do?

Table 5. Medications at a Glance

Although SSRIs are the mainstays of medication treatment for adolescent anxiety disorders, several other types of medications are sometimes prescribed as well. Following is a quick rundown of these medications.

Drug class	Specific medications	How they may work
Selective serotonin reuptake inhibitors	citalopram (Celexa) escitalopram (Lexapro) fluoxetine (Prozac) fluvoxamine (Luvox) paroxetine (Paxil) sertraline (Zoloft)	Affect the concentration and activity of a brain chemical called serotonin.
Serotonin–norepinephrine reuptake inhibitors	duloxetine (Cymbalta) venlafaxine (Effexor)	Affect the concentration and activity of two brain chemicals: serotonin and norepinephrine.
Tricyclic antidepressants	amitriptyline (Elavil) clomipramine (Anafranil) desipramine (Norpramin) doxepin (Sinequan) imipramine (Tofranil) maprotiline (Ludiomil) nortriptyline (Pamelor) protriptyline (Vivactil) trimipramine (Surmontil)	Affect the concentration and activity of two brain chemicals: serotonin and norepinephrine.
Benzodiazepines	alprazolam (Xanax) chlordiazepoxide (Librium) clonazepam (Klonopin) clorazepate (Tranxene) diazepam (Valium) lorazepam (Ativan) oxazepam (Serax)	May enhance levels of a brain chemical called gamma-amino-butyric acid.
Mood stabilizers	carbamazepine (Tegretol) lamotrigine (Lamictal) valproic acid (Depakote)	May enhance or inhibit various brain chemicals, depending on the drug.
Atypical antipsychotics	aripiprazole (Abilify) clozapine (Clozaril) olanzapine (Zyprexa) quetiapine (Seroquel) risperidone (Risperdal) ziprasidone (Geodon)	May enhance or inhibit various brain chemicals, depending on the drug.

- How soon should we see results?
- When and how often should my teen take the medication?
- How long should my teen take it?
- Will my teen need to limit any activities while taking the medication?
- Will my teen need to avoid alcohol, other drugs, or certain foods?
- What are the possible side effects of the medication?
- What should I do if these side effects occur?
- What number should I call if I have any questions or concerns?

Encouraging Adherence

Some teens simply don't like the idea of taking medicine. As one parent says, "My son sees medication as a crutch. He feels like he should be able to handle his own problems." Certainly, your teen's attitude is one factor that should be considered when evaluating treatment options. But there may be times when medication seems necessary and you need to encourage your teen to adhere to the treatment plan.

Often, what helps most is educating your teen about the disorder. Once he or she knows more about the biological roots of an anxiety disorder, it makes it much easier to understand the rationale for taking medication. Listen to your teen's concerns and beliefs about the treatment, and try to clear up any misconceptions. If you're uncertain about the facts yourself, don't hesitate to ask your teen's treatment provider.

Another common objection to medication is the side effects. All drugs have the potential to cause unwanted effects in addition to the desired ones. These vary from person to person, so it's important to monitor how your teen reacts to the prescribed dose of a particular drug. Your teen's doctor should discuss potential side effects when first writing a prescription. Make sure you know in advance how to manage mild problems and when to call the doctor right away. Always let the doctor know about any severe, unexpected, or especially worrisome symptoms that arise after your

Your teen's doctor should discuss potential side effects when first writing a prescription

teen starts taking a medication. Mild side effects often go away on their own in a few days. If the side effects are more severe, the doctor may be able to change the drug or dosage.

Some teens are willing to give medication a try, but become discouraged when they don't see immediate improvement. Make sure your teen starts out with a realistic idea of how long it will take to see benefits. In the case of SSRIs, for example, it can take four to six weeks for the full effects to be felt. Impress on your teen that it's important to keep taking the medication as prescribed throughout this whole period unless the doctor says otherwise. If an SSRI proves to be effective, it's usually continued for at least 6 to 12 months and sometimes longer. Other antidepressants that are prescribed for anxiety operate on a similar timeframe.

Antianxiety Drugs

You may wonder why depression-relieving medications are the leading drugs for treating adolescent *anxiety* disorders. The reason is that it seems that anxiety and depression involve many of the same changes in brain chemicals. Drugs that target these brain chemicals often work for either disorder—or both, if they're present concurrently.

Most medications that are known to specifically target anxiety fall into a category called benzodiazepines. These medications act more rapidly than antidepressants. In fact, many people who take benzodiazepines feel better almost immediately. But research on the use of these medications in young people with anxiety disorders is sparse, and the results have been mixed. Also, none of the benzodiazepines has been specifically approved for use in children or adolescents.

Benzodiazepines can potentially cause side effects such as daytime drowsiness and decreased mental alertness. They also interact dangerously with alcohol, which is an issue with many teenagers. As a result, benzodiazepines usually aren't the first choice as a solo treatment for adolescents. Nevertheless, they may still be useful for some teens.

Many parents are understandably concerned about the addictive potential of benzodiazepines. In general, these medications need to be used over a period of 8 to 12 weeks before they lead to physical dependence. One sign of dependence is tolerance—in other words, the need to take more and more of the drug to achieve the same therapeutic effect as before. If people stop taking the drug too abruptly, they may also experience unpleasant withdrawal symptoms, such as increased anxiety, shakiness, headache, dizziness, trouble sleeping, loss of appetite, and, in extreme cases, seizures. However, when benzodiazepines are prescribed for the appropriate diagnosis and their use is monitored by a physician, there is usually very little risk of abuse or dependence. The exception to this may be individuals who already have a problem with abuse of or dependence on another substance.

One more medication approved for the treatment of anxiety disorders is buspirone (BuSpar). This medication is thought to work in part by enhancing the activity of serotonin, so its mechanism of action is actually more like that of SSRIs than of benzodiazepines. As with SSRIs, studies have found that buspirone helps relieve both anxiety and depression in adults. Unfortunately, there is not enough research to be clear about its effectiveness in young people. However, there are clinical reports of its usefulness in teens who have not responded to other types of medications.

Dealing with Insurance Issues

Locating high-quality treatment for your teen is one thing. Paying for it can be quite another. Many families have no insurance coverage at all for mental health services, while others who do have insurance may find that the coverage is woefully inadequate. Health plans often impose tight restrictions on mental health benefits, such as severely limiting the number of treatment sessions that are covered. Some plans also require higher copayments and deductibles for mental health services than for other types of health care, and other plans set lower annual and lifetime spending caps.

In 1996, the U.S. Congress passed the Mental Health Parity Act, which was intended to help equalize the way that mental and physical illnesses are covered under health insurance. This law prohibits group health plans from placing annual or lifetime dollar limits on mental health benefits that are lower than those for medical or surgical benefits. Unfortunately, there are many loopholes. For one thing, the law allows group health plans to exclude mental health benefits altogether if they choose. It only applies to plans that elect to include some mental health coverage in their benefits package. For another thing, the law doesn't apply to group health plans sponsored by employers with fewer than 51 workers. Nor does it apply to health insurance that you purchase on your own as an individual. In addition, it doesn't ban health plans from using tactics that skirt the spirit of the law, such as limiting the number of covered visits for mental health services, even if the plan doesn't impose similar limits for medical and surgical visits.

In addition to this federal legislation, 34 states to date have enacted their own mental health parity laws. The state laws often have significant coverage gaps of their own, however. For the last several years, a number of organizations—including the National Alliance on Mental Illness and the National Mental Health Association—have been lobbying to get more comprehensive legislation passed.

Besides private insurance, the other major source of financial help when paying for treatment is Medicaid. This public insurance program, paid for by a combination of federal and state funds, provides health and mental health care to low-income individuals who meet eligibility criteria. To find out more about Medicaid eligibility, check your local phone book government pages, or visit the Centers for Medicare and Medicaid Services website (www.cms.hhs.gov).

Since Medicaid has strict financial eligibility requirements, most middle-class families don't qualify. Yet these same families often have inadequate insurance coverage for mental health services, so they often wind up footing much of the bill themselves. Not surprisingly, many parents say that finding the money to pay for their teen's treatment is a concern. "Most of the things we've done for Jeff were not insured," says one mother. "Every time we see the psychiatrist, it costs $170 a visit, and insurance pays $35. When we see the psychologist, it's the same thing. And we've got a good policy, too, but this is an area the insurance companies just aren't interested in."

The results of a recent survey sponsored by the Annenberg Foundation Trust at Sunnylands highlight the problem. Of 506

What Does It Cost?

Treatment costs vary widely, but these are typical figures. Be aware, though, that fees may be higher in some parts of the country.

- Therapist in private practice—$60 to $200 per hour. Psychiatrists and psychologists generally charge more than other mental health professionals.
- Private clinic—$50 to $200 per hour. Individual therapy may be more expensive than group therapy. Some nonprofit clinics allow families with limited financial resources to pay reduced fees.
- Community mental health center—$5 to $50 for families with limited financial resources. Those who qualify for government medical assistance pay no fee.
- Medication—$32 to $128 per month on average for a generic antidepressant, or up to $279 per month on average for a brand-name antidepressant. The cost of doctor appointments is extra.

primary care physicians surveyed nationwide, 58% said they felt that lack of adequate insurance hindered the ability of young people to get the mental health treatment they need. While there's no easy solution to this problem, you can make the most of whatever mental health coverage your family has by learning more about how to navigate the insurance system.

ABCs of HMOs

If your family does have mental health coverage—either through private insurance or Medicaid—chances are good that you'll be dealing with some type of managed care organization. Managed care

You can make the most of whatever mental health coverage your family has by learning more about how to navigate the insurance system.

is a system designed to control health care costs. There are several different kinds of managed care plans:

- Health maintenance organization (HMO)—A type of managed care plan in which most of the health care providers are on the HMO staff. When it comes to mental health care, however, some HMOs contract with outside providers. In such cases, you typically must get a referral from a primary care doctor at the HMO before seeing the mental health care provider.
- Preferred provider organization (PPO)—In this type of managed care plan, you may choose from a network of health care providers who have contracts with the PPO. You're less likely to need a referral from a primary care doctor to gain access to a mental health care provider.
- Point of service (POS) plan—This type of plan is similar to a traditional HMO or PPO. However, you also have the option of seeking care from providers outside the HMO or PPO network. If you choose to go out of network, you'll be required to pay a higher copayment or deductible.

Try, Try Again

If you ever submit a claim and the managed care company declines to pay it, don't give up too soon. You have the right to file an appeal if you believe that a claim has been unfairly turned down. Here's how the process works: Whenever a claim is submitted, someone on the staff of the managed care company reviews it to see whether it meets two criteria. First, the treatment being provided must be covered under the health plan. And second, the treatment must be deemed "medically necessary"—in other words, medically appropriate and necessary to meet the patient's health care needs. If both standards are met, payment

Picking a Health Plan

If you have a choice among different managed care health plans, be sure to compare the benefit packages carefully. These are some factors to consider when thinking about mental health coverage:

- Does the plan exclude any mental health diagnoses or services?
- Does the plan impose a waiting period or deny coverage for preexisting conditions?
- If your teen already has a mental health care provider, is he or she in the plan's network?
- If you'll be looking for a new provider, does the network include several near your home?
- Do any of these providers have expertise in treating anxiety disorders? If so, are they accepting new patients?
- How much are copayments and deductibles—in other words, your out-of-pocket expenses?
- Are there limits on the number of therapist sessions or doctor visits allowed per year?
- Is there a cap on the amount your plan will pay for mental health care in a 12-month period?
- Are there any restrictions on the medications that are covered?

for the treatment is authorized. But if either standard is failed, payment can be denied.

When a claim is denied, that decision is often based on the medical necessity standard. For example, a health plan may provide for a certain number of therapist visits per year, and a therapist or doctor may believe that the person needs therapy. Nevertheless, the managed care company can decide not to pay for the visits because they aren't deemed medically necessary by the company's reviewer. In this situation, you're entitled to file an appeal, which gives you a chance to make your case for why the treatment really is needed. Enlist the help of the mental health care provider who originally recommended the treatment. He or she is ethically bound to assist with the appeals process. If the situation is urgent, ask the provider to request an expedited appeal.

In less urgent cases, the appeals process can take some time. Make sure you understand your financial obligations if the provider starts the treatment during that period and the appeal is ultimately unsuccessful. Should your first appeal be denied, ask for written notification of the reasons. This notice should include a list of conditions that would have to be met for the treatment to be approved. You can always appeal again. In fact, most managed care companies offer three or four levels of appeal. Since each appeal is heard by a different set of people, you may have more success on the second or third try.

Most managed care companies offer three or four levels of appeal.

If your insurance is provided by an employer, the human resources department may be able to help you sort out benefits problems. If your family is covered by Medicaid, the state may have an ombudsman—a person or program charged with investigating and resolving consumer complaints. Medicaid recipients can also request a "fair hearing" from the state. The process varies from state to state, so contact your local Medicaid office for further information.

Solving Problems at School

Education is another area in which parents can be strong advocates for teens with anxiety disorders. By nature, teachers tend to be caring individuals. Most genuinely want to help, but they may not realize that there's a problem or know what to do about it. By sharing what you've learned, you can educate the educators. With greater knowledge will probably come enhanced understanding and cooperation.

Some teens with anxiety disorders have few, if any, problems in the classroom. If your teen seems to be struggling at school or with homework, though, it's time to initiate a dialogue with the teacher and perhaps other key school personnel. Before scheduling the first meeting, talk to your teen. Discuss any privacy concerns he or she may have, but also discuss your concerns about the effect that anxiety seems to be having on your teen's behavior or performance in the classroom. If you believe that your teen's teacher has a legitimate need to know about the anxiety disorder, clearly explain your reasons. Then have a discussion about what information you will share—and what you won't. You can allay many of your teen's worries simply by being open, honest, and willing to take his or her privacy preferences into account.

Once you sit down with a teacher, you'll want to talk about the specific symptoms each of you is observing and how they may be affecting your teen at school. But in order to put those symptoms in context, you may need to provide some general background information about your teen's anxiety disorder. "We provided the teachers with all kinds of brochures and written information," says Candace, the mother of two sons with OCD and Tourette's syndrome. Her sons' teachers had dealt with both disorders before, but they still seemed appreciative of the reading material. "Teachers are intellectually curious," says Candace. "I think they approach it in terms of, 'Oh, this is really interesting.' So they're very willing to read the material and discuss it."

Rather than limiting themselves to written information, some parents have also brought a mental health professional along to meetings. Maria, whose daughter has both OCD and social anxiety disorder, says, "I would bring in a psychologist for, like, 45 minutes to talk with her teachers each year." This approach can be expensive, since you'll have to pay for the professional's time. But Maria believes it helped the teachers develop better strategies for working with her daughter.

Carefully listening to teachers can also provide you with helpful information. Your teen's teachers have a chance to observe behavior that you may not see at home, and many have a wealth of experience when it comes to handling learning and behavioral problems. Take advantage of their expertise. If you approach the meeting as an opportunity for respectful give-and-take, you're more likely to get a positive response. After all, you're in this together, so it's to your mutual benefit to collaborate on finding solutions. On the other hand, if you take an aggressively demanding tone, the teachers' defenses will go up, and you're likely to end up in an antagonistic posture.

Carefully listening to teachers can also provide you with helpful information.

After that initial meeting, stay in touch throughout the year. Make it easy for teachers to reach you when a problem or question arises. If you're rarely home, for instance, make sure the teachers have your mobile or work phone number in addition to your home one. For your part, if you become aware of a problem, don't hesitate to bring it up. The sooner you address minor issues, the less likely they are to turn into major crises. Often, your teen's treatment provider may suggest problem-solving strategies that you can pass along to the teacher. This can make life easier for the teacher, and it helps ensure good coordination between your efforts at home and those in the classroom.

Don't forget to mention when things go *right*, too. Like everyone else, teachers like to know that their efforts are noticed and

Teaming Up with Teachers

When it comes to your teen's education, teachers are your most valuable allies. Below, parents of teens with anxiety disorders share their A+ tips for building positive relationships with teachers.

- Become a familiar face at the school. "I volunteered a lot when he was in elementary school. When he got to middle school, I started working again, so I couldn't volunteer as much. But I stayed on the PTA board, and I'm involved as much as possible. When you're there a lot and you volunteer, teachers are more willing to go out of their way to help you."
  —Mother of a 14-year-old

- Stay in touch by phone and email. "Since e-mail, it's much easier to communicate with his teachers. They can just shoot me an e-mail and tell me when he's not doing his work."
  —Mother of a 14-year-old

- Make good use of parent-teacher meetings. "If you're going to a meeting at the school, know ahead of time what it is that you want to accomplish. Do your homework, and come to the meeting prepared."   —Father of a 16-year-old

appreciated. When a teacher goes the extra mile to help your teen, a thank-you note or small homemade gift will not only make the teacher's day, but also cement your relationship.

Many anxiety-related school issues can be handled efficiently and effectively through informal channels. But if your teen has more severe, pervasive, or long-lasting problems, you may want to consider more formal options. In the United States, there are two main laws that cover educational services for students with disabilities: the Individuals with Disabilities Education Improvement Act of 2004 (IDEA) and Section 504 of the Rehabilitation Act of 1973.

The New IDEA

IDEA is the nation's special education law, the first version of which was enacted three decades ago. In December 2004, a major revision of the act was signed into law, and most of the new provisions were slated to go into effect in July 2005. At the time this book went to press, this newest version of IDEA had not yet been implemented, and final regulations were still being drafted. For the latest updates, see the websites of the Council for Exceptional Children and National Dissemination Center for Children with Disabilities.

In order to qualify for special educational services under IDEA, students must have a disability that impacts their ability to benefit from general educational services. Several different categories of disability are specified by the law. Students with anxiety disorders may qualify under one of two categories: serious emotional disturbance or other health impairments. Traditionally, the "serious emotional disturbance" label has been applied to students who have long-lasting, severe problems with an emotional basis, such as a tendency to develop fears associated with personal or school problems, or an inability to build and maintain satisfactory relationships with peers and teachers. This certainly sounds as if it could fit students with severe, chronic anxiety disorders. But the term serious emotional disturbance has a negative ring that many parents and teens find offensive. In some schools, the term has come to be regarded as a synonym for troublemaker. By extension, teachers may see anxiety-related behaviors as signs of willful disobedience rather than symptoms of a real illness.

The "other health impairments" label has traditionally been given to students with acute or chronic health problems that adversely affect their educational performance. This category is used for students who have general medical conditions, such as asthma and diabetes, that interfere with their ability to function at school. However, it's also used for those affected by mental and behavioral disorders with a biological basis, such as attention-deficit hyperactivity disorder. Since anxiety disorders also have biological underpinnings, they seem to fit into this category as well. Some parents and teens prefer the more neutral-sounding label. They believe that it reduces the stigma attached to both students and families, and it encourages educators to view anxiety disorders more compassionately.

IDEA in Action

The first step to accessing services under IDEA is to request an evaluation to determine a student's eligibility. An evaluation can be requested by either parents or school personnel. If the school initiates the request, your consent will be sought. If you initiate the request, the school must either conduct a full, individual evaluation, or give you notice of its refusal and let you know your rights. Assuming that an evaluation is done, the latest version of IDEA says that it generally must be completed within 60 days of the date when the school receives your consent. But there's an exception: The law allows states to establish shorter or longer timeframes through legislation or regulations. Once the evaluation is complete, you'll be notified of the results. If your child is deemed ineligible for services, and you disagree, you can request an independent educational evaluation by an outside party.

If your child is determined to be eligible for services, the next step is to develop a written individualized educational plan (IEP). Among other things, this key document states a student's present level of achievement and performance, establishes annual goals for the student, describes how progress toward the goals will be measured, and outlines the services that the student needs. The IEP is developed at a meeting by a team that is composed of parents, general education and special education teachers, and other school personnel. You and the school can also invite additional people who have relevant knowledge or expertise—for instance, a therapist, advocate, or educational consultant—to attend the IEP meeting. In addition, your child can attend the meeting if he or she wants to be there.

The IEP will specify any necessary educational accommodations—changes that help a student overcome or work around a disability. For example, a student whose anxiety about making mistakes leads to slow classroom performance might be given extra time to take tests. The IEP also specifies the student's placement—for example, in a regular classroom, a special education classroom, or a special school for students with a particular disability. The guiding principle of IDEA is to place students in the "least restrictive environment"—in other words, the one that allows them to be educated alongside their peers without disabilities to the greatest extent possible while still meeting their individual needs. For most students with anxiety disorders, this means being placed in a regular classroom with a few accommodations and supports. However, if the anxiety symptoms are very severe and persistent, or if there are other problems in addition to the anxiety disorder, the IEP might specify another placement, such as a part-time or full-time special education class.

Assuming that you agree with the accommodations and placement spelled out in your child's IEP, you'll sign it, and the plan will go into effect. You and the rest of the IEP team will then meet periodically to review your child's progress, make any needed changes in services, and develop new goals. If you disagree with the IEP, though, don't sign. At this point, you can try to hammer out a compromise with the IEP team. If that doesn't work, IDEA provides for mediation—a meeting between parents, school officials, and an impartial third party who helps both sides try to reach an acceptable agreement. When all else fails, you can request an impartial due process hearing—a more formal meeting in which you and the school district are each given a chance to present your case before a hearing officer, who makes a decision based on requirements in the law. Prior to the hearing itself, the latest version of IDEA requires a resolution session, a preliminary meeting at which you and the school district take one more stab at resolving your points of contention.

Even when all goes smoothly, the IEP process can be time-consuming and burdensome. Before starting down this path, you need to decide whether the benefits are likely to outweigh the hassles. Many teens with anxiety disorders need few, if any, accommodations in the classroom. And the accommodations that *are* required frequently are only necessary for a short time until treatment begins to work. The IEP process really isn't intended for such students.

But for those with more extensive and long-lasting needs, having an IEP opens the door to a wide range of educational and support services that are provided by the school district at no expense to the parents, regardless of the family's income level. Even students with disabilities whose parents choose to enroll them in private schools are entitled to receive free educational evaluations and services comparable to those provided to students in public schools.

Mike's daughter, an eleventh-grader with severe OCD and social anxiety disorder, has an IEP. At the school district's expense, she currently attends a private school for students with emotional and behavioral problems, where she receives a lot of

Comfortable Accommodations

Educational accommodations and modifications fall into five main categories. In some cases, such changes are only needed for a short time until treatment begins to work.

- Scheduling—Example: Allotting extra time to complete tests for a student with generalized anxiety disorder who takes too long because of being overly perfectionistic.
- Setting—Example: Allowing a presentation to be made to a small group rather than to the whole class for a student with social anxiety disorder who has an intense fear of public speaking.
- Materials—Example: Providing copies of the teacher's lecture notes to a student with OCD who has trouble taking notes by hand because of a handwriting compulsion.
- Instruction—Example: Temporarily reducing the difficulty of assignments for a student with post-traumatic stress disorder who has just gone through another traumatic experience.
- Student response—Example: Accepting check marks instead of filling in circles on tests for a student with OCD who gets hung up on trying to fill in the circles perfectly.

one-on-one attention in a small-class setting. "I've always felt the IEP was to her benefit," Mike says. "In the beginning, I was concerned about her being labeled. But the thing was, her problems were so severe that she would have been labeled no matter what. Having an IEP just gave her a tool to be successful."

"Her problems were so severe that she would have been labeled no matter what. Having an IEP just gave her a tool to be successful."

Another Option

If your student doesn't qualify for an IEP, Section 504 of the Rehabilitation Act of 1973 offers another option. To qualify for a 504 plan, students must have a physical or mental impairment that substantially limits one or more major life activities—an easier standard to meet than the IEP requirements. Although developing a 504 plan involves its own set of procedures, the process is sometimes more expeditious than that for an IEP. In theory, a 504 plan can be used to provide a wide range of educational services. In practice, since schools don't get extra funding under Section 504 the way they do under IDEA, this type of plan is usually reserved for students with impairments who need relatively inexpensive accommodations—and that describes many teens with anxiety disorders.

Carla's daughter, Beth, had a 504 plan in high school that provided her with extra time for taking tests. Overall, Beth was an excellent student, but tests were a continual source of tremendous anxiety for her. "It was really helpful for her to have that 504 plan," says Carla. "I saw a huge difference in her anxiety level once the plan was in place." To some extent, just knowing that the plan was there when she needed it seemed to help, since Beth never took advantage of another accommodation that would have allowed extra time for homework, too. Carla, who had initially resisted the idea of the plan, now believes it was a very wise move.

Support for You and Your Teen

Which teachers at your teen's school are most receptive to working with parents? Which managed care companies have the most extensive network of providers in your area? Which local therapists and psychiatrists do parents and teens recommend? Among your best sources for answers to these questions and many more are other parents of adolescents with anxiety disorders. Chances are, they've faced some of the same problems you're facing right now, and many are eager to pass along the smart solutions they've found.

You've seen the statistics showing that up to 5% of young people have an anxiety disorder at any given time. But at the end of a long, exhausting day, it's easy to feel as if you're the only parent in the world who has ever had to deal with the sometimes maddening, sometimes heartbreaking behavior of a teen with an anxiety disorder. Left unchecked, that sense of isolation can lead to stress and depression. On the other hand, knowing that other parents have bounced back from similar frustration and despair can be hugely reassuring.

Family and friends are usually great sources of moral support, but they may not always understand what you're going through when it comes to your teen's symptoms. That's where support groups come in. "It's so helpful just to meet other people who are struggling with the same issues," says one mother. "One of the first things I did was join an online support group, and it was absolutely wonderful," says another. In addition to emotional support, she appreciates the practical coping tips she gets there. As she puts it, "I never knew how much I *didn't* know about OCD as a social worker until my own kid was diagnosed. I really learned a lot from the group. And as time went on, I was able to help others, too."

"One of the first things I did was join an online support group, and it was absolutely wonderful."

To find a nearby support group, contact the Anxiety Disorders Association of America. Your doctor, therapist, or clergy person may know of groups in your area, too. Online support groups are another alternative. While many busy parents love the 24/7 access, be aware that the quality of these groups can vary widely. Look for a moderated group to reduce spam and other inappropriate messages. Some of the best online groups have input from highly qualified professionals as well as parents.

Support groups can also be valuable for the teens themselves. Keep in mind that there's a difference between a support group (which is a group of people with a common bond who get together to share emotional support, practical advice, and sometimes educational resources) and group therapy (which involves a group of people with similar emotional or behavioral problems who meet with a therapist to work on specific therapeutic goals). A support group won't take the place of treatment for an anxiety disorder. But it can be a source of much-needed encouragement and nonjudgmental acceptance from peers.

One mother says her 13-year-old daughter wasn't sure quite what to think at first about being diagnosed with OCD. "She said, 'I know other people who have migraines, and I know other people who have asthma, but I don't know anybody else who has this.' So we looked around and found out that there was a kids' OCD support group at a hospital in our area. It's not exactly close by; it's almost an hour's drive away. But we made the drive once a week for a while, just so she would know other kids who had OCD."

Incidentally, you may have noticed a common thread running through many of the parents' comments in this chapter. They talk about driving long distances, spending large sums of money, and going to considerable trouble to help their teens with anxiety disorders. It's precisely that kind of determination and dedication that often makes the critical difference in a young person's life. One parent whose 16-year-old son was recently diagnosed with an anxiety disorder puts it this way: "We're a strong family, and we're not going to just lay down when there's a problem. I'm going to try my hardest as a father to get the best treatment for my kid. We're not sure yet exactly what he's going to have to do, but we'll help him every step of the way. We'll get through this together."

Chapter Eight

Call to Action: Fighting Stigma, Empowering Your Teen

"My daughter isn't shy at all about talking about her anxiety," says one mother. "I know that she has told some of her friends that she has this illness, and she's very comfortable with that. For people my age, mental illness was considered very shameful, and everyone hid it. But it's a whole new world out there."

Unfortunately, not every family has met with such enlightened reactions. Another mother says, "When we first told the teachers that my son was on Zoloft [the brand name for sertraline, a common medication for treating anxiety disorders], they were quite alarmed. A lot of people just don't understand these things well enough, so they get freaked out."

A third parent says, "Telling the grandparents was hard. When my brother-in-law was a teenager, he had clinical depression, and his father actually said, 'No kid of mine is going to see a shrink.' Of course, he doesn't understand why his grandsons are getting psychiatric care, either. I know people who just didn't tell the relatives, and in some families, that's probably the best policy."

Anxiety disorders are the most common mental disorders in young people. Yet they are still widely misunderstood. Relatives, friends, teachers, and society at large are sometimes quick to condemn and slow to grasp the causes and consequences of intense, persistent anxiety. As one frustrated parent puts it, "They don't have a lot of empathy for it, because they don't understand it."

Dispelling Societal Myths

As the parent of a child with an anxiety disorder, you're on the front line of the battle against stigma. Perhaps the most important thing you can do is to counter misinformation with facts. Most people would never judge someone harshly for having diabetes or arthritis. Yet these same people seem to forget that the brain is part of the body, and like other organs, susceptible to disease and dysfunction. Often, they're less judgmental about anxiety disorders once they realize that the emotional and behavioral symptoms are related to physiological changes in the brain.

When you hear people using derogatory terms or making insensitive jokes about mental illness, let them know that you find this unacceptable. Showing a little sensitivity isn't just a matter of "political correctness." It's a matter of basic respect, and your teen deserves no less. Given that an estimated 44 million Americans experience a mental disorder of some kind in any given year, you may be surprised by how much support is on your side once you start to speak up.

The harmful consequences of stigma don't end with hurt feelings. The stereotypes that people hold about those with anxiety disorders can limit your teen's social, educational, and future occupational opportunities. And unfortunately, the fear of such repercussions deters many teens and families from seeking mental health care. Despite the fact that anxiety disorders are highly treatable, only about one-third of people who have an anxiety disorder ever get the treatment they need.

When teens are regarded by others as if there is something terribly "wrong" with them, many start to believe it. They may unfairly blame themselves for their anxiety, or they may start to view themselves as weak and ineffectual. Such attitudes, in turn, may further discourage appropriate help-seeking. Research has shown that there is a strong relationship between feeling shame and avoiding treatment.

Promoting Self-Acceptance

Despite the difficulties an anxiety disorder can cause, there are many good reasons to feel optimistic. You have the chance to start your adolescent down a more hopeful path now by getting treatment for your teen and promoting a positive self-image. It's all in the way you explain things. One mother whose 13-year-old has obsessive-compulsive disorder (OCD), including a compulsion to do things in sets of three, put it to him this way: "I told him it's okay with *me* if you have to do these things three times. Anyone who knows you and loves you won't care. But if it's to the point where it's getting in your way and it's making you upset, then we've got to do something. That's why we're going to the doctors: so that it can stop bothering *you*."

Another way to empower your teen is by standing up assertively to the prejudice of others. When you do this, you serve as a positive role model that your teen can emulate. In addition, you let your teen know, by your deeds as well as your words, that your love and acceptance aren't contingent on some standard of "perfection" that no one can achieve. Few things give a more powerful boost to a teen's self-esteem than this kind of unwavering parental support.

One of the most difficult challenges all parents of adolescents face is gradually letting go. Yet this may also be the ultimate expression of confidence in your teen's ability to overcome anxiety. "It's scary to let your child grow up, and anxiety makes it a little scarier," says the mother of a 16-year-old. "I worry that she'll be leaving home in a year and a half, and then there won't be two of us watching out for her. But I'm also proud of her for being so independent. You can be there to support them and help them, but they reach a point where they're too old for you to impose your ideas on them. In the end, you have to let them go."

> "It's scary to let your child grow up, and anxiety makes it a little scarier."

The Next Leg of Your Journey

If your teen is still in the process of getting diagnosed or receiving treatment, the future may still seem very uncertain. "It's hard for me to look ahead," says the mother of a 13-year-old who was diagnosed with OCD fairly recently. "We're so deep in the swirl of the moment that it's hard to see what's coming two *months* from now, much less where he'll be in two years or five years or ten years."

Yet the future will arrive, and there's no reason why it can't be a promising one. Jack's daughter, Lindsay, began experiencing panic attacks a decade ago, when she was 11 years old. At first, Lindsay's parents took her to see the family doctor, who brushed off their concerns, advising them to just ignore the panic attacks and wait for her to outgrow them. But the longer they waited, the worse their daughter's anxiety grew. By the time Lindsay's parents took her to see a mental health specialist, her symptoms had become quite severe. It was a dark period for the whole family, although Jack says there was one notable bright spot: "When Lindsay was ill, she turned to playing the piano and writing songs as a sort of self-therapy."

With professional treatment and lots of moral support from her parents, Lindsay's symptoms slowly abated, but her love of music remained. At age 21, she's following in the footsteps of her father, himself a musician, by pursuing a career as a singer-songwriter. Looking back, Jack says, "The worst thing in the world is to see your child suffering." He urges other parents to trust their instincts and seek help from a qualified mental health professional sooner rather than later. Beyond that, he advises, "Just never give up. Find ways to manage their symptoms so that they have breathing space to express themselves. Help them take small steps at their own pace. And always let them know that your love is limitless."

"Help them take small steps at their own pace. And always let them know that your love is limitless."

Appendix

Diagnostic Criteria

The *DSM-IV-TR* (short for *Diagnostic and Statistical Manual of Mental Disorders*, Fourth Edition, Text Revision) is a manual published by the American Psychiatric Association. Mental health professionals use it for diagnosing all kinds of mental disorders. The following diagnostic criteria for various anxiety disorders, presented here in alphabetical order, have been adapted from that manual.

Generalized Anxiety Disorder

1. Excessive anxiety and worry that occur more days than not for at least six months. The anxiety and worry are focused on a number of different events or activities.
2. The person finds it difficult to control the worry.
3. The anxiety and worry are associated with at least three of the following symptoms:
   a. Restlessness or edginess
   b. Tiring easily
   c. Difficulty concentration or mind going blank

   d. Irritability
   e. Muscle tension
   f. Insomnia or restless sleep
  4. The anxiety and worry aren't limited to the typical concerns of another anxiety disorder.
  5. The symptoms cause marked distress, or they significantly impair a person's ability to function in social, academic, or other important settings.
  6. The symptoms are not caused by alcohol or drug abuse, a general medical condition, or the side effects of a medication.

Obsessive-Compulsive Disorder

  1. The presence of either obsessions or compulsions.
   a. Obsessions involve all of the following symptoms:
    i. Repeated thoughts, impulses, or mental images that are intrusive and inappropriate, and that cause marked anxiety or distress.
    ii. These thoughts are not simply excessive worries about real-life problems.
    iii. The person tries to ignore or suppress the thoughts, or the person tries to neutralize them with some other thought or action.
    iv. The person recognizes that the obsessive thoughts are a product of his or her own mind.
   b. Compulsions involve all of the following symptoms:
    i. Repeated behaviors (for example, hand washing, putting things in a certain order, checking to make sure a particular action has been done) or mental acts (for example, praying, counting,

repeating words silently). The person feels driven
to perform these actions in response to an
obsession or according to rigid rules.

  ii. These behaviors are aimed at preventing or
reducing distress, or at preventing some dreaded
event from occurring. However, the behaviors are
either clearly excessive or not linked in a realistic
way to the threat they are meant to neutralize.

2. At some point, the person recognizes that the obsessions
or compulsions are excessive or unreasonable.

3. The obsessions or compulsions lead to at least one of
the following reactions:
   a. Marked distress
   b. Time-consuming thoughts or behaviors that take up
   more than an hour a day
   c. Significant interference with the person's normal
   routine or social relationships
   d. Significant impairment of the person's ability to
   function in social or academic settings

4. The symptoms are not caused by alcohol or drug abuse,
a general medical condition, or the side effects of a
medication.

Panic Disorder

1. Repeated, spontaneous panic attacks, which are distinct
periods of intense fear or distress. The panic attacks start
suddenly, peak within ten minutes, and involve at least
four of the following symptoms:
   a. Pounding heart or rapid heart rate
   b. Sweating

      c. Trembling

      d. Shortness of breath or a suffocating feeling

      e. Choking sensation

      f. Chest pain

      g. Nausea

      h. Dizziness or faintness

      i. Feelings of unreality or detachment from oneself

      j. Fear of losing control or "going crazy"

      k. Fear of dying

      l. Numbness or tingling

      m. Chills or hot flushes

2. At least one of these symptoms has occurred for a month or more following a panic attack:

      a. Persistent worry about having future attacks

      b. Worry about the implications or consequences of the attack (for example, concern about losing control, "going crazy," or having a heart attack)

      c. Significant change in behavior related to the attack

3. The symptoms are not caused by alcohol or drug abuse, a general medical condition, or the side effects of a medication.

Post-Traumatic Stress Disorder

1. Past exposure to a traumatic event that led to intense feelings of fear, helplessness, or horror. The event involved at least one of these elements:

      a. Actual or threatened death or serious injury

      b. A threat to the person's physical integrity (for example, child sexual abuse)

   c. Witnessing the death, serious injury, or threat to physical integrity of another

   d. Learning about the sudden, unexpected death or serious injury of a close loved one

2. The traumatic event is repeatedly reexperienced in at least one of the following ways:

   a. Recurring memories of the event that are intrusive and distressing

   b. Recurring nightmares about the event

   c. Flashbacks in which the person, while awake, acts or feels as if the event is happening again

   d. Intense emotional distress when exposed to triggers that remind the person of the event

   e. Intense physical reactions when exposed to triggers that remind the person of the event

3. Persistent avoidance of things associated with the traumatic event as well as emotional numbing. These reactions are evidenced by at least three of the following symptoms:

   a. Efforts to avoid thinking, feeling, or talking about the event

   b. Efforts to avoid people, places, or activities that bring back memories of the event

   c. Inability to recall some important part of the event

   d. Reduced interest or participation in activities that were once enjoyed

   e. Feeling detached or estranged from others

   f. Restricted range of emotions (for example, the inability to feel love)

   g. Sense of a foreshortened future (for example, not expecting to live past 25)

4. Persistent signs of increased arousal. This arousal is evidenced by at least two of the following symptoms:

    a. Difficulty falling or staying asleep

    b. Irritability or outbursts of anger

    c. Difficulty concentrating

    d. Constant vigilance

    e. Exaggerated startled response

5. The symptoms last for more than a month.

6. The symptoms cause marked distress, or they significantly impair the person's ability to function in social, academic, or other important settings.

Separation Anxiety Disorder

1. Excessive, age-inappropriate anxiety about being separated from the home or people to whom the individual is emotionally attached. This is evidenced by at least three of the following symptoms:

    a. Repeated, excessive distress when separation from the home or primary caregivers occurs or is anticipated

    b. Persistent, excessive worry about losing or having harm befall the primary caregivers

    c. Persistent, excessive worry that an untoward event, such as getting lost or being kidnapped, will lead to separation from a primary caregiver

    d. Persistent reluctance to go to school or someplace else because of fear of separation

    e. Persistent, excessive fear or reluctance to be alone or spend time apart from significant adult figures

    f. Persistent reluctance to sleep away from home or go to sleep without a primary caregiver nearby

    g. Repeated nightmares about separation

    h. Repeated complaints of physical symptoms—such as headaches, stomachaches, nausea, or vomiting—when separation from primary caregivers occurs or is anticipated

2. The symptoms last for at least four weeks.
3. The problem starts before age 18.
4. The symptoms cause marked distress, or they significantly impair the person's ability to function in social, academic, or other important settings.

Social Anxiety Disorder

1. Extreme, persistent fear of one or more social situations in which the individual is exposed to unfamiliar people or possible scrutiny by others. The person fears that he or she will act in a way that leads to embarrassment or humiliation. In young people, at least some of the feared situations must involve peers.
2. Exposure to the feared social situation almost always provokes anxiety. In the most extreme cases, this anxiety may take the form of a panic attack.
3. The person recognizes that the fear is excessive or unreasonable.
4. The feared social situation is avoided, or it is endured only with great anxiety or distress.
5. The avoidance, distress, or worry caused by the disorder leads to at least one of the following reactions:

    a. Significant interference with the person's normal routine or social relationships

    b. Significant impairment of the person's ability to
       function in social or academic settings
    c. Marked distress about having the disorder
6. In individuals under age 18, the symptoms last for at
   least six months.
7. The symptoms are not caused by alcohol or drug abuse,
   a general medical condition, or the side effects of a
   medication.

Specific Phobia

1. Extreme, persistent fear that is excessive and
   unreasonable. This fear is triggered by the presence or
   anticipation of a specific object or situation (for
   example, dogs, blood, enclosed places, or heights).
2. Exposure to the feared object or situation almost always
   provokes immediate, extreme anxiety or panic.
3. The person recognizes that the fear is excessive or
   unreasonable.
4. The feared object or situation is avoided, or it is
   endured only with great anxiety or distress.
5. The avoidance, distress, or worry caused by the phobia
   leads to at least one of the following reactions:
    a. Significant interference with the person's normal
       routine or social relationships
    b. Significant impairment of the person's ability to
       function in social or academic settings
    c. Marked distress about having the phobia
6. In individuals under age 18, the symptoms last for at
   least six months.

Glossary

5-HTT   A gene that helps regulate the amount of serotonin in the brain. A variant of the gene that produces low levels of serotonin has been linked to certain anxiety disorders.

accommodation   A change that helps a person overcome or work around a disability.

acute post-traumatic stress disorder   Post-traumatic stress disorder that lasts from one to three months.

acute stress disorder   An anxiety disorder that develops following exposure to a traumatic event and lasts no more than one month. It is characterized by reexperiencing the trauma, avoidance, increased arousal, and dissociative symptoms.

adrenal glands   Glands located just above the kidneys. Their hormones help regulate many physiological functions, including the body's stress response.

adrenocorticotropic hormone (ACTH)   A hormone released by the pituitary gland.

agoraphobia   Avoidance associated with panic disorder. It is characterized by fear and associated avoidance of places or situations from which escape might be difficult or help might not be available in the event of a panic attack.

amygdala   A structure inside the brain that plays a central role in the fear response.

anorexia nervosa   An eating disorder in which people have an intense fear of becoming fat, leading them to severely restrict what they eat, often to the point of near starvation.

antidepressant   A medication used to prevent or relieve depression.

anxiety   The apprehensive anticipation of future danger or misfortune.

anxiety disorder   Any of a group of disorders characterized by excessive fear or worry that is recurrent or long-lasting. The symptoms of the disorder cause distress or interfere with day-to-day activities.

attention-deficit hyperactivity disorder (ADHD)   A disorder characterized by a short attention span, excessive activity, or impulsive behavior.

atypical antipsychotic   One of the newer antipsychotic medications. Some atypical antipsychotics are also used as mood stabilizers.

autonomic nervous system   The portion of the nervous system that controls involuntary functions of internal organs.

axon   The sending branch on a nerve cell.

basal ganglia   A cluster of neurons within the brain that plays a key role in movement and behavior.

behavioral inhibition   A type of temperament in which individuals are typically irritable as infants, fearful as toddlers, and shy and wary as school-aged children.

benzodiazepine   An antianxiety medication that is thought to raise levels of gamma-amino-butyric acid in the brain.

beta-blocker   A medication that is usually prescribed for high blood pressure or heart problems. Beta-blockers are also occasionally prescribed for performance anxiety.

body dysmorphic disorder   An obsessive-compulsive spectrum disorder in which people become so preoccupied with an imagined defect in their appearance that it causes serious distress or significant problems in their everyday life.

bulimia nervosa   An eating disorder in which people binge on large quantities of food, then purge by forced vomiting, laxative or diuretic abuse, or excessive exercise.

buspirone (BuSpar)   An antianxiety medication that increases serotonin activity in the brain while decreasing dopamine activity.

cerebral cortex   The part of the brain that is responsible for higher-order thought processes, such as language and information processing.

chronic post-traumatic stress disorder   Post-traumatic stress disorder that lasts longer than three months.

classical conditioning   A mental association that is formed by pairing a previously neutral stimulus with a stimulus that produces an innate response. Over time, the previously neutral stimulus becomes able to bring on the response by itself.

cognitive-behavioral therapy (CBT)   A form of therapy that helps people recognize and change self-defeating thought patterns as well as identify and change maladaptive behaviors.

comorbidity   The coexistence of two or more disorders in the same individual.

compulsion   A repetitive behavioral or mental act that a person feels driven to perform in response to an obsession or according to rigid rules.

conduct disorder   A disorder characterized by a repetitive or persistent pattern of having extreme difficulty following rules or conforming to social norms.

corticotropin-releasing factor (CRF)   A hormone released by the hypothalamus.

cortisol   A hormone released by the adrenal glands that is responsible for many of the physiological effects of stress.

depression   A disorder that involves either being in a low mood or irritable nearly all the time, or losing interest or enjoyment in almost everything.

***Diagnostic and Statistical Manual of Mental Disorders*, Fourth Edition, Text Revision (*DSM-IV-TR*)**   A manual that mental health professionals use for diagnosing mental disorders.

disruptive behavior disorder   A disorder that leads to very troublesome behavior; for example, attention-deficit hyperactivity disorder, conduct disorder, or oppositional defiant disorder.

domestic violence   Violence that occurs within the context of an intimate relationship, such as marriage or dating.

dopamine   A neurotransmitter that is essential for movement and also influences motivation and perception of reality.

eating disorder   A disorder characterized by serious disturbances in eating behavior. People may severely restrict what they eat, or they may go on eating binges, then attempt to compensate by such means as self-induced vomiting or misuse of laxatives.

emotional processing theory   A theory of anxiety disorders in which fear is defined as a cognitive structure that serves as a blueprint for escaping or avoiding danger. Different anxiety disorders reflect different structures.

exposure and response prevention (EX/RP)   A form of cognitive-behavioral therapy that is used to treat obsessive-compulsive disorder. The exposure part involves having people confront the thoughts or situations that provoke their obsessional distress, while the response prevention part means voluntarily refraining from using compulsions to reduce their distress during these encounters.

exposure and ritual prevention   See exposure and response prevention.

exposure therapy   A form of cognitive-behavioral therapy in which people are taught to systematically confront a feared object or situation under safe conditions. The goal is to allow them to learn that the feared stimuli are not actually dangerous.

extinction   The weakening of a response that has been learned through classical conditioning.

eye movement desensitization and reprocessing (EMDR)   A form of therapy for post-traumatic stress disorder that combines elements of exposure therapy with directed shifts in attention.

gamma-amino-butyric acid (GABA)   A neurotransmitter that inhibits the flow of nerve signals in neurons by blocking the release of other neurotransmitters. It is thought to help quell anxiety.

generalized anxiety disorder (GAD)   An anxiety disorder characterized by excessive anxiety and worry over a number of different things.

generalized social anxiety disorder   Social anxiety disorder that occurs in most social situations.

group therapy   Therapy that brings together a group of people with similar emotional or behavioral problems, who meet with a therapist to work on specific treatment goals.

health maintenance organization (HMO)   A type of managed care plan in which members must use health care providers who work for the HMO.

hippocampus   A brain structure involved in emotion, learning, and memory.

hypochondriasis   An obsessive-compulsive spectrum disorder in which people become preoccupied with the idea that they have a serious illness, based on their misinterpretation of harmless bodily signs and sensations.

hypothalamic-pituitary-adrenal (HPA) axis   A body system comprised of the hypothalamus, pituitary gland, and adrenal glands along with the substances these structures secrete.

hypothalamus   Part of the brain that serves as the command center for the nervous and hormonal systems.

individualized educational plan (IEP)   A written educational plan for an individual student who qualifies for services under IDEA.

Individuals with Disabilities Education Improvement Act of 2004 (IDEA)   The federal special education law, which applies to students who have a disability that impacts their ability to benefit from general educational services.

insomnia   Difficulty falling or staying asleep.

irritable bowel syndrome   A stress-related digestive disorder in which the large intestine doesn't function properly, leading to symptoms such as abdominal cramps, bloating, constipation, or diarrhea.

learning disorder   A disorder that adversely affects a person's performance in school or ability to function in everyday situations that require reading, writing, or math skills.

least restrictive environment   The setting that allows a student with a disability to be educated alongside peers without disabilities to the greatest extent possible while still meeting his or her individual needs.

managed care   A system designed to control health care costs.

Medicaid   A public insurance program, paid for by a combination of federal and state funds, that provides health and mental health care to low-income individuals who meet eligibility criteria.

medical necessity   A standard used by managed care plans in determining whether or not to pay for a health care service. To satisfy this standard, the service must be deemed medically appropriate and necessary to meet a patient's health care needs.

mental health parity   A policy that attempts to equalize the way that mental and physical illnesses are covered by health plans.

mood stabilizer   A medication that helps even out extreme mood swings.

neuron   A cell in the brain or another part of the nervous system that is specialized to send, receive, and process information.

neurotransmitter   A chemical that acts as a messenger within the brain.

norepinephrine   A neurotransmitter that helps regulate arousal, sleep, and blood pressure. Excessive amounts of norepinephrine may trigger anxiety.

obsession   A recurrent thought, impulse, or mental image that is perceived as intrusive and inappropriate, and that provokes anxiety and distress.

obsessive-compulsive disorder (OCD)   An anxiety disorder characterized by recurrent, uncontrollable obsessions or compulsions.

obsessive-compulsive spectrum disorder   Any of a group of disorders that resemble obsessions or compulsions and may respond to some of the same treatments as obsessive-compulsive disorder.

oppositional defiant disorder   A disorder characterized by a persistent pattern of unusually frequent defiance, hostility, or lack of cooperation.

panic attack   A sudden, unexpected wave of intense fear and apprehension that is accompanied by physical symptoms, such as a rapid heart rate, shortness of breath, or sweating.

panic disorder   An anxiety disorder characterized by the repeated occurrence and fear of spontaneous panic attacks. The fear results from the belief that such attacks will result in catastrophes, such as having a heart attack.

pediatric autoimmune neuropsychiatric disorders associated with streptococcal infections (PANDAS)   An uncommon childhood form of obsessive-compulsive disorder that is brought on by a strep infection.

performance anxiety   A limited form of social anxiety in which the excessive fear relates to performing a specific task in front of others.

pituitary gland   A small gland located at the base of the brain. Its hormones control other glands and help regulate growth, metabolism, and reproduction.

placebo   A sugar pill that looks like a real medication, but does not contain an active ingredient.

point of service (POS) plan   A type of managed care plan that is similar to a traditional health maintenance organization (HMO) or preferred provider organization (PPO), except that members can also use providers outside the HMO organization or PPO network in exchange for a higher copayment or deductible.

post-traumatic stress disorder (PTSD)   An anxiety disorder that develops following exposure to a traumatic event. Symptoms include reexperiencing the trauma, avoidance and emotional numbing, and increased arousal.

preferred provider organization (PPO)   A type of managed care plan in which members may choose from a network of providers who have contracts with the PPO.

prefrontal cortex   The front part of the cerebral cortex. It is involved in complex thought, problem solving, and emotion.

protective factor   A characteristic that decreases a person's likelihood of developing a disorder.

psychiatrist   A medical doctor who specializes in the diagnosis and treatment of mental illnesses and emotional problems.

psychological debriefing   A mental health service that is provided to survivors immediately after a traumatic event. The goal is to help survivors understand their feelings, reduce their distress, and prepare for what they may face in the future.

psychologist (clinical)   A mental health professional who provides assessment and therapy for mental and emotional disorders.

randomized controlled trial   A study in which participants are randomly assigned to a treatment group or a control group. The control group typically receives either a placebo, a nonspecific psychotherapy, or standard care. This study design allows researchers to determine which changes in the treatment group over time are due to the treatment itself.

receptor   A molecule that recognizes a specific chemical, such as a neurotransmitter. For a chemical message to be sent from one nerve cell to another, the message must be delivered to a matching receptor on the surface of the receiving nerve cell.

reuptake   The process by which a neurotransmitter is absorbed back into the sending branch of the nerve cell that originally released it.

risk factor   A characteristic that increases a person's likelihood of developing a disorder.

school refusal   Extreme reluctance to go to school.

Section 504   A section of the Rehabilitation Act of 1973 that applies to students who have a physical and mental impairment that substantially limits one or more major life activity.

selective mutism   An uncommon disorder in which children who are physically and mentally capable of speaking completely refuse to talk in certain social situations.

selective serotonin reuptake inhibitor (SSRI)   An antidepressant that affects the concentration and activity of serotonin in the brain. SSRIs are widely prescribed for anxiety disorders as well as depression.

separation anxiety disorder   An anxiety disorder, found mainly in children, that involves excessive anxiety about being separated from the parent or home.

serotonin   A neurotransmitter that helps regulate mood, sleep, appetite, and sexual drive. Low levels of serotonin have been linked to both anxiety and depression.

serotonin–norepinephrine reuptake inhibitor (SNRI)   An antidepressant that affects the concentration and activity of serotonin and norepinephrine in the brain. SNRIs are prescribed for anxiety disorders as well as depression.

side effect   An unintended effect of a drug.

social anxiety disorder   An anxiety disorder characterized by marked fear in social situations where the person is exposed to unfamiliar people or possible scrutiny by others.

social phobia   See social anxiety disorder.

specific phobia   An anxiety disorder characterized by an intense fear that is focused on a specific animal, object, activity, or situation, and that is out of proportion to any real threat.

stigma   Stereotyping, prejudice, and discrimination that are directed toward a particular group of people.

strep throat   An infection of the throat caused by streptococcus bacteria. It is characterized by a sore throat, fever, and swollen lymph nodes in the neck.

substance abuse   The continued use of alcohol or other drugs despite negative consequences, such as dangerous behavior while under the influence or substance-related personal, social, or legal problems.

support group   A group of people with a common problem who get together to share emotional support, practical advice, and sometimes educational resources.

synapse   The gap that separates nerve cells.

temperament   A person's inborn tendency to react to events in a particular way, which remains relatively stable over time.

thalamus   A brain structure that acts as a relay station for incoming sensory information.

tic   A sudden, rapid, repetitive movement or vocalization.

Tourette's syndrome   A neurological disorder characterized by frequent, multiple tics.

transporter   A molecule that carries a chemical messenger, called a neurotransmitter, back to the nerve cell that originally sent the message.

trichotillomania   An obsessive-compulsive spectrum disorder in which people feel driven to pull out their own hair, leading to noticeable hair loss.

tricyclic antidepressant   An older class of antidepressant that affects the concentration and activity of serotonin and norepinephrine in the brain. Tricyclic antidepressants are prescribed for anxiety disorders as well as depression.

Further Reading and Resources

Organizations

About Our Kids
New York University Child Study Center
577 First Avenue
New York, NY 10016
(212) 263-6622
www.aboutourkids.org

Agoraphobics Building Independent Lives
400 West 32nd Street
Richmond, VA 23225
(804) 353-3964
www.anxietysupport.org

American Academy of Child and Adolescent Psychiatry
3615 Wisconsin Avenue N.W.
Washington, DC 20016-3007
(202) 966-7300
www.aacap.org

American Psychiatric Association
1000 Wilson Boulevard, Suite 1825
Arlington, VA 22209-3901
(703) 907-7300
www.psych.org

American Psychological Association
750 First Street N.E.
Washington, DC 20002-4242
(800) 374-2721
www.apa.org

Anxiety Disorders Association of America
8730 Georgia Avenue, Suite 600
Silver Spring, MD 20910
(240) 485-1001
www.adaa.org

Association for Behavioral and Cognitive Therapies
305 Seventh Avenue, 16th Floor
New York, NY 10001
(212) 647-1890
www.aabt.org

Bazelon Center for Mental Health Law
1101 15th Street N.W., Suite 1212
Washington, DC 20005
(202) 467-5730
www.bazelon.org

Council for Exceptional Children
1110 N. Glebe Road, Suite 300
Arlington, VA 22201
(703) 620-3660
www.cec.sped.org

Federation of Families for Children's Mental Health
1101 King Street, Suite 420
Alexandria, VA 22314
(703) 684-7710
www.ffcmh.org

Food and Drug Administration
5600 Fishers Lane
Rockville, MD 20857
(888) 463-6332
www.fda.gov

Freedom From Fear
308 Seaview Avenue
Staten Island, NY 10305
(718) 351-1717
www.freedomfromfear.org

International Society for Traumatic Stress Studies
60 Revere Drive, Suite 500
Northbrook, IL 60062
(847) 480-9028
www.istss.org

National Alliance for the Mentally Ill
Colonial Place Three
2107 Wilson Boulevard, Suite 300
Arlington, VA 22201-3042
(800) 950-6264
www.nami.org

National Association of School Psychologists
4340 East West Highway, Suite 402
Bethesda, MD 20814
(301) 657-0270
www.nasponline.org

National Center for Post-Traumatic Stress Disorder
U.S. Department of Veterans Affairs
VA Medical Center (116D)
215 N. Main Street
White River Junction, VT 05009
(802) 296-6300
www.ncptsd.org

National Child Traumatic Stress Network
Substance Abuse and Mental Health Services Administration
5600 Fishers Lane
Parklawn Building, Room 17C-26
Rockville, MD 20857
(301) 443-2940
www.nctsnet.org

National Dissemination Center for Children with Disabilities
P.O. Box 1492
Washington, DC 20013
(800) 695-0285
www.nichcy.org

National Institute of Mental Health
6001 Executive Boulevard, Room 8184, MSC 9663
Bethesda, MD 20892-9663
(866) 615-6464
www.nimh.nih.gov

National Mental Health Association
2001 N. Beauregard Street, 12th Floor
Alexandria, VA 22311
(800) 969-6642
www.nmha.org

National Mental Health Information Center
Substance Abuse and Mental Health Services Administration
P.O. Box 42557
Washington, DC 20015
(800) 789-2647
www.mentalhealth.org

Obsessive-Compulsive Foundation
676 State Street
New Haven, CT 06511
(203) 401-2070
www.ocfoundation.org

Sidran Institute
200 E. Joppa Road, Suite 207
Towson, MD 21286
(410) 825-8888
www.sidran.org

Books

Chansky, Tamar E. *Freeing Your Child From Obsessive-Compulsive Disorder.* New York: Crown, 2000.

Dacey, John S., and Lisa B. Fiore. *Your Anxious Child: How Parents and Teachers Can Relieve Anxiety in Children.* San Francisco: Jossey-Bass, 2000.

Dornbush, Marilyn P., and Sheryl K. Pruitt. *Teaching the Tiger: A Handbook for Individuals Involved in the Education of Students With Attention Deficit Disorders, Tourette Syndrome or Obsessive-Compulsive Disorder.* Duarte, CA: Hope Press, 1995.

Fitzgibbons, Lee, and Cherry Pedrick. *Helping Your Child With OCD: A Workbook for Parents of Children With Obsessive-Compulsive Disorder.* Oakland, CA: New Harbinger, 2003.

Foa, Edna B., and Reid Wilson. *Stop Obsessing! How to Overcome Your Obsessions and Compulsions* (rev. ed.). New York: Bantam, 2001.

Merrell, Kenneth W. *Helping Students Overcome Depression and Anxiety: A Practical Guide.* New York: Guilford Press, 2001.

Monahon, Cynthia. *Children and Trauma: A Guide for Parents and Professionals.* San Francisco: Jossey-Bass, 1993.

Penzel, Fred. *Obsessive-Compulsive Disorders: A Complete Guide to Getting Well and Staying Well.* New York: Oxford University Press, 2000.

Rachman, Stanley, and Padmal de Silva. *Panic Disorder: The Facts* (2nd ed.). New York: Oxford University Press, 2004.

Rapee, Ronald M., Susan H. Spence, Vanessa Cobham, and Ann Wignall. *Helping Your Anxious Child: A Step-by-Step Guide for Parents.* Oakland, CA: New Harbinger, 2000.

Rapoport, Judith L. *The Boy Who Couldn't Stop Washing: The Experience and Treatment of Obsessive-Compulsive Disorder.* New York: Dutton, 1989.

Spencer, Elizabeth DuPont, Robert L. DuPont, and Caroline M. DuPont. *The Anxiety Cure for Kids: A Guide for Parents.* Hoboken, NJ: John Wiley and Sons, 2003.

Wagner, Aureen Pinto. *What to Do When Your Child Has Obsessive-Compulsive Disorder: Strategies and Solutions.* Rochester, NY: Lighthouse Press, 2002.

Wagner, Aureen Pinto. *Worried No More: Help and Hope for Anxious Children.* Rochester, NY: Lighthouse Press, 2002.

Waltz, Mitzi. *Obsessive-Compulsive Disorder: Help for Children and Adolescents.* Sebastopol, CA: O'Reilly, 2000.

Wilens, Timothy E. *Straight Talk About Psychiatric Medications for Kids.* New York: Guilford Press, 2004.

Multimedia

Obsessive Compulsive Foundation. *OCD in the Classroom: A Multi-Media Program for Parents, Teachers and School Personnel.* New Haven, CT: Obsessive Compulsive Foundation, undated.

Websites

American Psychiatric Association, Healthy Minds site, www.healthyminds.org
American Psychological Association, Trauma site, www.apa.org/topics/
    topictrauma.html
Madison Institute of Medicine, Post-traumatic Stress Disorder site,
    http://ptsd.factsforhealth.org
Madison Institute of Medicine, Social Anxiety Disorder site,
    http://socialanxiety.factsforhealth.org
National Institute of Mental Health, PANDAS site,
    http://intramural.nimh.nih.gov/pdn/web.htm
National Institute of Mental Health, Pediatric Obsessive Compulsive Disorder
    site, http://intramural.nimh.nih.gov/pocd
Obsessive Compulsive Foundation of Metropolitan Chicago,
    www.ocfchicago.org
PTSD Alliance Resource Center, www.ptsdalliance.org

Resources for Adolescents

Fiction

Buffie, Margaret. *Angels Turn Their Backs*. Tonawanda, NY: Kids Can Press, 1998.
Hesser, Terry Spencer. *Kissing Doorknobs*. New York: Laurel Leaf Books, 1998.
Tashjian, Janet. *Multiple Choice*. New York: Henry Holt, 1999.

Websites

Annenberg Foundation Trust at Sunnylands with the Annenberg Public Policy
    Center of the University of Pennsylvania, MindZone, www.fhidc.com/
    annenberg/copecaredeal
Nemours Foundation, TeensHealth, www.teenshealth.org
Obsessive-Compulsive Foundation, Organized Chaos, www.ocfoundation.org/1001

Resources for Related Problems

Attention-Deficit Hyperactivity Disorder

Attention-Deficit Disorder Association, (484) 945-2101, www.add.org
Children and Adults with Attention-Deficit/Hyperactivity Disorder, (800) 233-
    4050, www.help4adhd.org

Depression

Book

Evans, Dwight L., and Linda Wasmer Andrews. *If Your Adolescent Has Depression or Bipolar Disorder: An Essential Resource for Parents.* New York: Oxford University Press with the Annenberg Foundation Trust at Sunnylands and the Annenberg Public Policy Center at the University of Pennsylvania, 2005.

Websites

Depression and Bipolar Support Alliance, (800) 826-3632, www.dbsalliance.org

National Alliance for Research on Schizophrenia and Depression, (800) 829-8289, www.narsad.org

Eating Disorders

Book

Walsh, B. Timothy, and V. L. Cameron. *If Your Adolescent Has an Eating Disorder: An Essential Resource for Parents.* New York: Oxford University Press with the Annenberg Foundation Trust at Sunnylands and the Annenberg Public Policy Center at the University of Pennsylvania, 2005.

Websites

Academy for Eating Disorders, (847) 498-4274, www.aedweb.org

Anorexia Nervosa and Related Eating Disorders, www.anred.com

National Association of Anorexia Nervosa and Associated Disorders, (847) 831-3438, www.anad.org

National Eating Disorders Association, (800) 931-2237, www.nationaleatingdisorders.org

Learning Disorders

International Dyslexia Association, (410) 296-0232, www.interdys.org

LD OnLine, www.ldonline.org

Learning Disabilities Association of America, (412) 341-1515, www.ldaamerica.org

National Center for Learning Disabilities, (888) 575-7373, www.ld.org

Substance Abuse

Alcoholics Anonymous, (212) 870-3400 (check your phone book for a local number), www.aa.org

American Council for Drug Education, (800) 488-3784, www.acde.org

Leadership to Keep Children Alcohol Free, (301) 654-6740, www.alcoholfreechildren.org

Narcotics Anonymous, (818) 773-9999, www.na.org
National Council on Alcoholism and Drug Dependence, (800) 622-2255,
    www.ncadd.org
National Institute on Alcohol Abuse and Alcoholism, (301) 443–3860,
    www.niaaa.nih.gov
National Institute on Drug Abuse, (301) 443-1124, www.drugabuse.gov
National Youth Anti-Drug Media Campaign, (800) 666-3332,
    www.mediacampaign.org
Partnership for a Drug-Free America, (212) 922-1560,
    www.drugfreeamerica.com
Substance Abuse and Mental Health Services Administration, (800) 662-4357,
    www.samhsa.gov

Tourette's Syndrome

Tourette Syndrome Association, (718) 224-2999, www.tsa-usa.org
Worldwide Education and Awareness for Movement Disorders,
    www.wemove.org

Resources for Trauma Recovery

National Center for Children Exposed to Violence, (877) 496-2238,
    www.nccev.org
National Center for Victims of Crime, (202) 467-8700, www.ncvc.org
National Clearinghouse on Child Abuse and Neglect Information, (800) 394-
    3366, nccanch.acf.hhs.gov

Bibliography

American Psychiatric Association. *Diagnostic and Statistical Manual of Mental Disorders* (4th ed., text revision). Washington, DC: American Psychiatric Association, 2000.

Evans, Dwight L., Edna B. Foa, Raquel E. Gur, Herbert Hendin, Charles P. O'Brien, Martin E. P. Seligman, and B. Timothy Walsh (eds.). *Treating and Preventing Adolescent Mental Health Disorders: What We Know and What We Don't Know.* New York: Oxford University Press with the Annenberg Foundation Trust at Sunnylands and the Annenberg Public Policy Center at the University of Pennsylvania, 2005.

Foa, Edna B., and Barbara Olasov Rothbaum. *Treating the Trauma of Rape: Cognitive-Behavioral Therapy for PTSD.* New York: Guilford Press, 1998.

Foa, Edna B., Terence M. Keane, and Matthew J. Friedman (eds.). *Effective Treatments for PTSD.* New York: Guilford Press, 2000.

Kearney, Christopher A. *Social Anxiety and Social Phobia in Youth: Characteristics, Assessment, and Psychological Treatment.* New York: Springer, 2005.

March, John S., and Karen Mulle. *OCD in Children and Adolescents: A Cognitive-Behavioral Treatment Manual.* New York: Guilford Press, 1998.

Morris, Tracy L., and John S. March (eds.). *Anxiety Disorders in Children and Adolescents* (2nd ed.). New York: Guilford Press, 2004.

Ollendick, Thomas H., and John S. March. *Phobic and Anxiety Disorders in Children and Adolescents: A Clinician's Guide to Effective Psychosocial and Pharmacological Interventions.* New York: Oxford University Press, 2004.

Rapee, Ronald M., Ann Wignall, Jennifer L. Hudson, and Carolyn A. Schniering. *Treating Anxious Children and Adolescents: An Evidence-Based Approach.* Oakland, CA: New Harbinger, 2000.

Silva, Raul R. (ed.). *Posttraumatic Stress Disorders in Children and Adolescents: Handbook.* New York: W. W. Norton, 2004.

Index

About the Authors

Edna B. Foa, Ph.D. is a Professor of Clinical Psychology in Psychiatry at the University of Pennsylvania and Director of the Center for the Treatment and Study of Anxiety. Dr. Foa has published several books and over 250 articles and book chapters and has lectured extensively around the world. Her work has been recognized with numerous awards and honors.

Linda Wasmer Andrews is a freelance science writer based in Albuquerque, New Mexico. She is the co-author of *If Your Adolescent Has Depression or Bipolar Disorder: An Essential Resource for Parents* and the author of nine books, including *Emotional Intelligence* (for young readers). Ms. Andrews is a regular contributor to *Self* magazine.